BUS

4/20/98

The Buck Starts Here:

The Beginner's Guide to Smart Financial Choices

BY LISA MURR CHAPMAN

Simon & Schuster

Published by
Kaplan Educational Centers and Simon & Schuster
1230 Avenue of the Americas
New York, New York 10020

Copyright © 1997, by Lisa Murr Chapman

Editor: Donna Ratajczak
Cover Design: Cheung Tai
Interior Page Design and Production: Bola Famuyiwa
Production Editor: Maude Spekes
Assistant Managing Editor: Brent Gallenberger
Managing Editor: Kiernan McGuire
Executive Editor: Del Franz

Special thanks to: Doreen Beauregard, Sarah Pearl, Jobim Rose, and Sumi Wong

For bulk sales to schools, colleges, and universities,
please contact:
Renee Nemire
Simon & Schuster Special Markets
1633 Broadway, 8th Floor
New York, NY 10019

Manufactured in the United States of America
Published Simultaneously in Canada

September 1997
10 9 8 7 6 5 4 3 2 1

Library of Congress Cataloging-in-Publication Data

    Chapman, Lisa Murr.
    The buck starts here : the beginner's guide to smart financial
      choices / by Lisa Murr Chapman.
    p.   cm.
    ISBN: 0-684-84172-X
    1. Finance, Personal.   I. Title
    HG179.C533   1997   97-26022
    332.024—dc21   CIP

ISBN: 0-684-84172-X

TABLE OF CONTENTS

Lisa Murr Chapman is an entrepreneur, real estate investor, and author. Her published books include *The Savvy Woman's Guide to Cars* (Bantam), *Country Stars Shine* (Eggman Publishing), and *Just For You* (Goldner & Associates). Ms. Chapman was the founder, chairwoman, and CEO of a health care business in Nashville that grew to over ten million dollars in annual revenues with eight offices in five states.

Ms. Chapman's professional awards and achievements include *Nashville Business Journal's* Executive of the Year and Small Business of the Year finalist awards, as well as inclusion in *Nashville Business and Lifestyle* magazine's list of "40 Under 40—Nashville's Emerging Leadership." Her business background includes seven years in sales and marketing, as well as six years in a variety of accounting capacities. Ms. Chapman received her undergraduate degree in accounting and her M.B.A. from the University of Houston.

$ECTION 1
Money Management Basics

CHAPTER 1

Your Cash in Motion: Money-Management Strategies

If you're like most people, especially most people in their 20s and 30s, you probably avoid making long-range money plans. And who could blame you? Right now your cash flow seems like a mere trickle. But consider the following statistics.

If you work 40 years and earn an average of $25,000 per year, you will have made $1 million. If you get annual raises of five percent, the $1 million explodes to $3 million. The question is, how much of it can you keep? Okay, you're not particularly interested in that right now because you're on a tight budget. Besides, once you get a real job, you'll be earning real money. So you'll worry about it then, right?

Wrong, wrong, wrong. The time to think about it is right now. Start today, with good judgment and smart choices. It doesn't matter if you don't have much money. Maybe you're at your first job after college, trying to furnish and apartment and pay off student loans on an entry-level salary.

Or maybe you're still in school, and feel that you don't have enough money to worry about. But as one financial aid officer at a large university in the southeast advises, "Students absolutely must have some kind of budget in place if they have a limited amount of cash each month." So whether you're still in school, or out there working already, keep thinking the smart way and lifelong financial security will inevitably follow. The secret is in actively managing your cash flow.

Your cash is constantly in motion. You get cash. You give cash. Every time you turn around, you are either taking money in or spending it. Most of us think that the challenge is simply how to get more. "If only I had an extra $200. I could . . . go out of town . . . get that jacket (or whatever your heart currently desires)." With that kind of thinking, you will never have enough money. You will always spend everything you make. The truth is, you will very likely spend more than you make and go into debt.

THE 10 PERCENT SOLUTION

Fancy financial planners all over the world charge their clients big bucks to implement one of the simplest little concepts imaginable. All of their complicated strategies for financial security and retirement planning can be boiled down to a simple practice that any parent could teach her six-year-old child. If you didn't learn about it when you were six, then now's a great time.

It's the Ten Percent Solution. Take ten percent right off the top of every dollar you take in and invest it. That's it.

So, you may be thinking that you can't afford it. You already have too many obligations. You need more money to be able to do that. You'll do it when you get out of school. You'll do it when you get a raise. Etcetera, etcetera, etcetera. Remember, you will never have enough money for all the things you want to do. Every time you get more money, there's always something else you'll want. It's very deceptive. We think we'll be happy when we just get that next wish. But by that time, there's always another one. Most people spend their lives chasing the next thing. They never understand this basic concept. And they wonder why they struggle so much financially.

Here's why you must start implementing the Ten Percent Solution immediately, regardless of how much money you are bringing in. It's human nature to prioritize buying things over saving money. Millions of people do it. Without a plan, that's what naturally happens every time. We simply want to have things more than we want to have money in savings.

By deciding to save ten percent off the top, you set up a system to beat the spiral of overspending and debt. By making the Ten Percent Solution your first priority, you force yourself to reprioritize other spending. You must pay yourself first, starting now.

Suppose you make $833.00 per month. By using the 10 percent solution and saving $83.33 of your salary, or $1,000 this year, in an investment yielding a 15 percent return, your accumulated savings is astonishing:

15 Percent Investment Return on $1,000

5 years	10 years	20 years
$2,010	$4,050	$16,380

As a general rule of thumb, a good investment is one that enables you to double your money every five to seven years. A similar financial growth concept should help drive home the importance of starting to save early in your life: If you contribute to a tax-deferred retirement account each year between the ages of 20 and 26 and never make another contribution, you will have more money at age 65 than if you wait until you're 26 and invest $2,000 every year for 40 years in a taxable investment.

If you're convinced that starting to save while you're young is a good idea, but you just can't see a clear way to accomplish it, then take a hard look at what you spend. No matter how much you bring in, you can find ten percent by studying your spending and making a few adjustments.

By the way, if you're carrying around the burden of high-interest debt, your ten percent solution "investment" is simply an investment in paying the debt down. Use the ten percent to reduce your debt until it is gone. Then continue to save ten percent in an investment that earns interest. For more information on handling debt, see section two of this book, Debt and Credit.

TRACK YOUR INCOME AND YOUR SPENDING

It's a fact that most people who don't have enough money don't know how much they spend each month, or on what. They're smart people with good educations. But they never took charge of their financial income and outgo. Sound ridiculous? Certainly you know how much you spent on rent or on your car. But how much did you really spend on entertainment? On fast food? On toiletries and cosmetics?

How often do you stop at the convenience store? Does it seem that the $20 you put in your wallet just disappears? If so, then you could make a powerful impact on your financial life by tracking your income and outgo daily. It doesn't have to be forever. Tracking your expenditures for only two months will give you a clear road map for finding ten percent for yourself. You'll be surprised at how painless it really is. The ten percent you find will actually be things that you can easily do without and probably won't even miss.

The Buck Starts Here

All you need to do is put a piece of paper and a pencil in your wallet. Every time you take out cash (or write a check, or use a credit card), jot down the item and the amount. Make a list of each expenditure every day. Include something as small and seemingly insignificant as a candy bar. Your list might look like this:

Monday, May 6

Expenditure	Amount	Category
Bagel and coffee	$ 1.37	Fast food
Cab	3.75	Transportation
Notebook	2.79	Education
Overdue library book fee	1.50	Education
Concert tickets	32.00	Entertainment
Lunch	4.62	Restaurant
Birthday card	2.80	Gifts
Groceries	26.31	Groceries
TOTAL	$75.14	

This list is your daily record. By compiling your daily records into a weekly record, and compiling your weekly records into monthly records, you have a concise snapshot of the exact uses of all your money. Your goal is to group your expenditures by type and develop categories for your expenditures in order to find out exactly where you spend money in each category.

The Sample Spending Tracker at the end of this chapter might help you formulate categories that fit your lifestyle. A recent graduate tried it for a month, then decided to make cuts from many of the categories. Even though she already lives with two roommates, she found that she spent much of her free cash on frivolous things. Just by spending a little less in several categories, she was able to save much more than the 10 percent she targeted to cut. Delighted by this, she set up a plan to pay down debts and establish a savings account for the first time in her life. Here's what her before and after budgets look like:

Sample Spending Tracker

Category:	Monthly Expenditures:	
	Before	*After*
Transportation		
car payments	$234	$234
insurance	76	76
gas	68	40
repairs and maintenance	50	50
cab/bus	0	0
other	0	0
Food		
groceries	324	240
fast food	106	40
restaurants	168	80
snacks	82	15
other	18	0
Housing		
rent/mortgage	140	140
insurance	0	0
telephone	54	30
utilities (heat, water, etcetera)	62	62
repairs and maintenance	0	0
other	0	0
Household		
furnishings	0	0
plants, etcetera	20	10
other	0	0

Education

tuition	—	—
books	—	—
supplies	—	—
fees	—	—
other	—	—

Clothing

garments	137	75
shoes	78	50
dry cleaning	34	26
laundry	20	20
other	0	0

Entertainment

tickets	42	21
admissions	12	12
hobbies	0	10
parties	36	20
gym or workout facility	35	35
cable T.V.	12	12
video rental	41	16
CDs and tapes	47	12
books and magazines	22	10
other	0	0

Health care

doctor and dentist	20	20
prescriptions	10	10
other	0	0

Personal		
haircut and treatment	72	36
manicure	22	0
massage	50	50
personal care products	88	50
other	0	0
Legal	0	0
Gifts	54	36
Donations	20	20
Clubs and organizations	20	20
Vacations	100	100
Other		
Other		
Other		
Other		
Other		
Other		
TOTAL:	$2,374	$1,678
	× 10%	
Targeted amount to cut:	$237	

In this example, ten percent of her total monthly expenditures was $237, but she actually found $696. In a year, that will add up to $8,352! How far would $8,352 go toward paying off your debt and increasing your savings? By simply curbing many unnecessary expenses, she essentially gave herself a big, fat raise. In addition to watching her spending, this is where she found many of her cutbacks:

Gas: Deciding to carpool to work when convenient and asking friends to chip in for gas when she drove on social occasions.

Groceries: Buying generic brands every time she could, eliminating the specialty and prepared "convenience items," and drastically reducing the snacks and soft drinks that weren't good for her anyway.

Fast food, restaurants and snacks: Cutting way back to just once a week and bringing food from home for lunch and snacks.

Clothing: Making selective purchases once per month instead of twice, and never buying on impulse. (She now makes herself go home without it; she returns the next day to purchase it, if she still really wants it after that cooling-off period.)

Video: Limiting her rentals to one tape per week.

Hair and nails: Finding a less expensive stylist and making appointments every six weeks instead of four.

Your objective now is to comb your daily detail list of expenditures to find relatively painless ways of cutting cash outgo. Cut or reduce items that are nonessential or can be accomplished in a less expensive way. Start with the easy things, such as entertainment. "I was astounded to learn how much money I wasted on fast food," one 24-year-old admitted. "When I quit going to the drive-through late at night, I had a lot more money left over at the end of the month."

COST-CUTTING TIPS

Some people find that avoiding teller machines for quick cash helps them harness their impulse spending. "When I don't have cash in my pocket, I don't spend it on junk," admitted Sherry, 20. Additional tips for saving money:

- Instead of paying health club fees, jog, walk, bike, or blade in the park. Partner with a friend to work out to a good exercise video.

- Scour the newspaper for free park concerts and events. Put them on your calendar and plan in advance to get friends together for them.

- Host a potluck dinner. Instead of cooking an expensive meal for guests, have everyone bring something while you provide the place.

- Make cards and gifts instead of buying them. Write a poem or give a picture of yourself.

- Write letters instead of making long-distance phone calls.

- Check out art galleries or exhibits. Visit museums.

- Take the bus instead of a cab. Consider riding your bike or walking.

- Find the $2.00 movie theater.

- Make pizza instead of ordering it.

- Use coupons.

- Borrow clothes for that special event instead of buying something new.

- Never go to the grocery store hungry.

DECIDE WHAT'S ESSENTIAL AND WHAT'S OPTIONAL

If you've identified easy ways to cut some spending, the next step is to identify the absolutely essential items. Highlight them on your list. After you've highlighted the essentials, everything that's not highlighted is a potential area to make more cuts. They may not be the easiest things, but they're not essential, either. They're all ways to consider cutting more fat.

CONSIDER CASH FLOW

Cash flow describes the timing of your receipt of cash versus your spending of cash. How much cash do you have available to you at any one time? Financial aid officers highly advise mapping out your cash flow on paper at the beginning of the term, "You must know exactly how much money you're getting and when you'll get it. This includes all sources such as family, financial aid, and income from your job. Then you can project your expenditures and exactly when you will make them. If you deposit a lump sum of cash in the bank at the beginning of the term, you can set it aside for a specific purpose."

The same holds true if you're working already. It's easy to track your income if you're employed at a steady job, but if you're temping or freelancing, tracking your income will be tougher and all the more important.

To help you get organized, we've included a sample spending tracking form at the end of this chapter.

Sample Spending Tracker

Category:	Monthly Expenditures:	
	Before	*After*
Transportation		
car payments		
insurance		
gas		
repairs and maintenance		
cab/bus		
other		
Food		
groceries		
fast food		
restaurants		
snacks		
other		
Housing		
rent/mortgage		
insurance		
telephone		
utilities (heat, water, etcetera)		
repairs and maintenance		
other		

Household
furnishings

plants, etcetera

other

Education
tuition

books

supplies

fees

other

Clothing

garments

shoes

dry cleaning

laundry

other

Entertainment
tickets

admissions

hobbies

parties

gym or workout facility

cable T.V.

video rental

CDs and tapes

books and magazines

other

Health care
    doctor and dentist

    prescriptions

    other

Personal
    haircut and treatment

    manicure

    massage

    personal care products

    other

Legal

Gifts

Donations

Clubs and organizations

Vacations

Other

Other

Other

Other

Other

Other

TOTAL: $ $

$\times\ 10\%$

Targeted amount to cut: $

CHAPTER 2

Make Your Money Go Farther

A spendthrift is a person who could also be described as a big spender, a high roller, or a person who tends to be careless with money. Are you a spendthrift? You probably already know the answer. But just to be sure, put yourself to the test:

THE SPENDTHRIFT QUIZ

1. Your idea of the perfect Friday night is:
   a. A good workout at the gym, followed by a beer or two with a friend.
   b. Being invited to dinner—by someone else!
   c. Shop till you drop.

2. You're dying to buy the latest rage in sunglasses, and they're on sale at the mall. The only problem is that even on sale, they're $95. You:
   a. Do some overtime at your job to raise some extra cash.
   b. Buy them. They're wonderful.
   c. Do nothing. You don't need another pair of sunglasses, anyway.
   d. Buy the $30 knock-offs instead.

3. Your birthday's coming up and it's a big one—twenty-one. You want to really blow it out. What do you do?
   a. Call two dozen friends and have them each bring something for a major party.
   b. Plan a whirlwind tour of the town; complete with limo and champagne.
   c. Invite a few of your closest friends for a weekend at a borrowed cabin retreat.

4. You have $400 for new winter clothes. You:
   a. Shop carefully, making sure the things you buy go with what you already have.
   b. Absolutely can't wait to go to the mall. And you take the credit card, too.
   c. Pay your bills instead (but you splurge on a new pair of shoes for $35).

5. You have a coupon for a free barbecue dinner. Your friend wants steak. Your solution is:
   a. Go for the steak—as long as your friend buys. Otherwise, you're eating barbecue.
   b. What the heck—go for the steak. Life's too short to sweat the small stuff.
   c. Offer to split the savings on barbecue with your friend.

The spendthrift would answer: 1.c, 2.b, 3.b, 4.b, and 5.b. If you had two or more spendthrift answers, you might take a closer look at your spending choices. The good news is that you'll find lots of ways to save money, and you may not even miss it too much. The easiest place to look is in the entertainment budget.

How to Save $200 or More (Painlessly) Without Changing the Way You Live

It really is possible to save money, even if you think you're at the bottom of the barrel now. You need to know only three basic concepts in order to spend less while maintaining your current lifestyle. Whenever you spend money on anything, ask yourself if you can:

1. Buy it for less.
2. Use less. Or
3. Make it last longer.

> "I used to hate thinking about money. But now it's a little game to see how much I can save. My roommate and I try to out-bargain each other. It's great fun," Maria, 23.

Apply these three principles to everyday expenditures. Brainstorm new ways to improve on every purchase you make. You can start right away with these examples:

40 Penny-Pinching Pointers

1. Buy in bulk, especially food.
2. Use coupons.
3. Search the discount bin at the grocery store for markdowns on slightly damaged boxes.
4. Don't shop at convenience stores.
5. Buy generic brands.
6. Don't buy convenience foods.
7. Shop thrift stores and consignment stores; try the ones in upscale neighborhoods for great bargains.
8. Watch for end-of-season and clearance sales.
9. Make meals from scratch.
10. Write letters instead of calling long distance.
11. Quit smoking.
12. Pack your lunch instead of eating out.
13. Get six friends together to swap clothing you no longer want or need.
14. Borrow best-sellers at the library or from friends instead of buying them.
15. Split bulk household staples with a friend (i.e., packages of soap, paper towels, pasta, etcetera).
16. Search out the best gas price and pump your own.
17. Have a friend cut your hair.
18. Shop for groceries on double coupon day.
19. Pop popcorn the old fashioned way instead of using those expensive microwave bags.
20. Eat loaded baked potatoes for dinner once a week (cost: about 35 cents each).
21. Install shareware from the public library instead of buying expensive computer software.
22. Post a swap offer on bulletin boards. Ask for what you need and offer what you have to swap.
23. Stop at the library to read magazines and newspapers instead of subscribing.
24. Shop at used book stores. Buy yard sale books to trade in for much more cash or credit.
25. Sell your old clothes at consignment shops.
26. Never, ever make impulse purchases.
27. Have the buffet for dinner at discount happy hours.
28. Don't buy clothing that needs to be dry cleaned.
29. Resole and recondition shoes instead of buying new ones.
30. Avoid disposable anything.
31. Develop film with lower-priced, mail-in envelopes (save half or more).
32. Ask for samples at the cosmetics counter.
33. Shop alone.
34. Shop with a list. If an item you want is not on the list, don't buy it.
35. Don't shop when you're hungry.
36. Buy merchandise with the best unit pricing (i.e., price per ounce, gallon, etcetera).
37. Shop at bakery thrift stores.
38. Never buy food out of a machine.
39. Return returnable bottles.
40. Walk there.

CLOTHES HORSE SENSE

Another great place to look for savings is in your clothing budget. With a little bit of creativity, you can radically slash your clothing expenditures and have better threads than you've ever had before. Competition for your clothing dollar is fierce. So go ahead and take advantage of it.

Finding quality merchandise at retailers, off-price stores, and outlets can be a bit of an art. But it's an art well worth pursuing, if only for the substantial financial rewards.

Department Stores

Traditional department stores sell seasonal clothing at very specific times of the year. You'll find the best sale prices just before the next season's merchandise arrives. Ask for sale dates at your favorite stores, because they vary from store to store and city to city. Generally, you'll catch the deepest markdowns about midway through a season. For example, lots of summer clothes are marked way down as early as July.

Department Store Clearance Centers

Lots of high-end department stores have jumped on the discount bandwagon by opening their own clearance centers for out-of-season merchandise. Their regular high quality stock is normally offered at discounts of up to 75 percent. During sales, you can find even deeper discounts. Imagine shopping at Neiman Marcus, Saks Fifth Avenue, and Nordstrom for one-fourth the price!

Off-Price Stores

For true deal hunters, especially during clearance sales, off-price stores offer a virtual feast of bargains. Manufacturers often dump slow-selling retail merchandise here, as well as overstocks and last season's clothes. Many times, the garments are first rate and quite stylish. But be prepared to look through lots of trash until you find your treasures. And inspect your treasures quite carefully for flaws, missing buttons, and correct sizing. If you find a problem, ask the manager for an additional discount. You're likely to get another 10 percent off the price.

Outlet Stores

Designer and factory outlet malls are popping up all over, especially at convenient interstate exits just outside of large cities. They're well worth the drive, with discounts of up to 75 percent off suggested retail. A lot of quality merchandise is found in them, with an increasingly current selection of seasonal apparel. As the popularity of outlet stores has increased, so have the prices. So shop carefully. It helps to know retail pricing of the same merchandise.

> Linda, 26, was one of many people who reported finding great bargains at thrift shops. "And lots of the 'finds' are vintage clothes with loads of character. I always get them cleaned first, so they feel fresh when I wear them for the first time."

FREE AND CHEAP GIFT AND HOLIDAY IDEAS

Holidays can easily be more frustrating and expensive than fun. Many people feel rushed, overburdened, and broke when it's all over. Especially when funds are short to begin with, it's tough to buy great gifts for all the people you care about. Just a few tips for advance planning and creative thinking can make the difference between embarrassment and gracious giving. This year, before the holidays start, give these ideas a try:

- With relatives and good friends, set spending limits together and challenge each other to have fun and be creative.

- Buy a gift for the entire family instead of individual gifts for each family member.

- Start a gift grab-bag with your family: Draw names and agree to spend within a range.

- Write a special letter describing how meaningful the recipient has been in your life.

- Give certificates for services that you can perform, such as baby-sitting, massage, or house cleaning.

- Make chocolate-covered pretzels or spice tea mix in pretty containers.

- Give beautiful holiday ornaments. Consider customizing them with a short message and the date in gold paint that you apply with a brush.

- Write a poem, haiku, or a song for a special person.

- Give a special picture of yourself or the recipient. Personalize it with a message and signature.

- Design personalized letterhead and run it off on bond on your computer.

- As gifts for folks on a fixed income, especially the elderly, note cards and postage stamps might be appreciated.

- Ask recipients what they might like to receive. Oftentimes they'll suggest something modestly priced.

- Special-interest books make thoughtful gifts. Be sure to inscribe it.

- Buy an autograph book and have friends and relatives of the recipient personalize it.

- Find magazines and newspapers at antique stores dated the month and year of the birth date of the recipient.

- Make closet and drawer sachets.

- Have friends personalize a T-shirt or sweatshirt for the recipient.

- Buy a blank book and customize each page with memories, phrases from favorite songs, photos, what you appreciate about the recipient, etcetera.

- Give a candy or cookie basket.

- Give international coffee beans in a festive mug.

- Press flowers and glue them to the front of plain note cards for a unique gift.

CHEAP THRILLS AND ENTERTAINMENT

You can save lots of money by excluding entertainment from your budget. But that's probably not very realistic for many people. You want to go out and have a good time. You want to get out of the house, join your friends, and enjoy the weekend. You can have fun and stick to your spending goals when you plan ahead and make a few changes. For instance, you might:

- Find the $2.00 theater or go to a matinee showing.

- Make pizza from scratch instead of buying it.

- Rent videos instead of going to the theater.

- Find two-for-one—or better—happy-hour deals.

- Start a weekly "game night" with your best friends.

- Ask your city's Visitor's Bureau for information on area parks, attractions, and for a calendar of events.

- Get a half-price coupon book from Entertainment Publications (1-800-477-3234) for your region or city.

- Don't order drinks and dessert at a restaurant.

- Eat only half of your restaurant meal and take the rest in a doggie bag for lunch tomorrow.

- Avoid nightspots that charge a cover.

CHAPTER 3

Instant Entrepreneur:
101 Ways to Earn Cash Fast

If you want to end up with more money, you can do one of two things: You can spend less, or you can earn more. The previous chapters dealt with spending less. This chapter is about earning more.

It's possible to develop your own business quickly, without incurring prohibitive startup expenses, by offering your services to the general public. The following list will help you brainstorm your own service-based business ideas for generating income quickly and with minimal investment. Services that people need right away and on a regular basis are the best bets. The key to getting calls for your service is your promotion activity. In order to create demand for your service, be creative in getting the word out. All of your ideas may be advertised or promoted to the general public very inexpensively, or even for free:

- Post fliers everywhere a bulletin board is available.

- Deliver fliers to nice homes door-to-door.

- Deliver fliers to small businesses in your area.

- Place classified ads in community newspapers.

Of course, not all of the services listed below will work for you. Find one or two that fit your interests and abilities and just give them a try! An ambitious sophomore at a small school in the northwest offered miniblind cleaning services. "Most maid services don't clean blinds. When I found that out, I put cards up at the grocery stores. Now all my customers come by word of mouth. I may build this business after I graduate." In addition to your promotional activities to reach the general public, a few ideas for reaching people who may be interested in the specific service are offered:

40 Services People Need

Service	Fee Range	Promotional Activities—Deliver Fliers to:
Auto detailing	$50–75	Auto parts stores, gas stations, used car lot managers
Aquarium cleaning	$25+	Pet shops and pet supply stores, busy office buildings
Baby-sitting	$5+/Hr	Day care centers, diaper services, bookstores
Dog sitting	$10+/Day	Veterinary offices, pet shops, pet supply stores
Care for elderly	$7+/Hr	Geriatric physician offices, home health supply stores
Computer assistance	$20+/Hr	Computer supply stores
Deejay service	$150+/Night	Party supply stores
Dog grooming	$20+	Pet shops, pet supply stores, and veterinarians
Exercise instructor	$20+/Hr	Weight loss centers, sporting goods stores, health clubs, massage centers
Diet consultant	$20+/Hr	Health and fitness centers, hair salons, massage centers
Garden care	$7+/Hr	Nurseries, lawn and garden centers, mowing services
Hair stylist	$20+	Health clubs, weight loss centers, beauty supply stores
House sitting	$20+/Day	Travel agencies, health clubs, hair salons
Grocery delivery	$10+	Busy office buildings, day care centers
House cleaning	$35+	Health clubs, hair salons, bookstores, day care centers
Ironing	Varies	Health clubs, hair salons, bookstores, day care centers

Janitorial	Varies	Office management companies, office supply stores, print shops
Laundry service	Varies	Health clubs, hair salons, bookstores, day care centers
Lawn care	$25+	Barber shops, health clubs, busy office buildings, lawn and garden centers
Manicurist	$20+	Busy office buildings, health clubs, massage centers, beauty supply stores
Massage	$35+	Health clubs, health food stores, travel agencies, hair salons, restaurants
Mechanic	Varies	Auto parts stores, gas stations
Painting	$10+/Hr	Hardware stores, property management companies
Plant care	Varies	Nurseries, property management companies
Pool/spa maintenance	Varies	Pool/spa supply stores, health clubs, hair salons
Reading service	$7+/Hr	Schools for the blind, sign language instructors
Research service	$10+/Hr	Bookstores, attorneys' offices, busy office buildings
Sharpening service: •Ice skates •Knives •Lawn mowers •Saws	Varies	Gourmet food stores, hardware stores, health clubs
Tutoring: •Academic •Achievement tests •Computer skills	Varies	School counselors, school supply stores, bookstores
Typesetting	$20+/Hr	Busy office buildings
Visiting service	Varies	Adult day care centers, home health care businesses

Wake-up service	$5+/Call	Health clubs
Window washing	Varies	Health clubs, hair salons, busy office buildings
Word processing	$2+/page	Copy/print shops, bookstores

GET PAID FOR DOING WHAT YOU ENJOY

Nothing beats doing what you enjoy! People will pay for something they can't do or don't have the time to do themselves. Think about your gifts and talents. Consider offering your services to others who don't have your skills and talents, but want or need them.

> "When I graduated from college, the job market was very tight, especially in my field. I needed to make some cash, but I also needed time for my job search. I had outgrown the fast-food-type jobs. And temp work was too infrequent.
>
> I found a part-time job that afforded to me the flexibility I sought. On weekends I entertained at childrens' birthday parties. I played dinosaurs, ninjas, clowns, and magicians, among others. The money was very good; I made about the same per hour as a lawyer at some fancy firm (of course I wasn't working 80-hour weeks). The work was also very satisfying. Kids aren't subtle in their appreciation. Their smiles mean a lot more to me than a cubicle with a view of the water cooler. After I started my 'real' job, I continued performing on weekends for the extra cash."—Robert, 26

Here are some more ideas to get you started:

Cashing In On Your Hobbies

Service	Fee Range	Promotional Activity—Deliver Fliers to:
Astrology charting	$50+/reading	Bookstores, New Age stores, health food stores
Auto maintenance and repair	Varies	Gas stations, auto parts stores

Bicycle tune-up/repair	$35+	Sporting goods stores, health clubs
Cake decorating	$20+	Party supply stores, flower shops, gift shops
Calligraphy	Varies	Art supply stores, stationary stores, print shops
Catering	Varies	Gourmet food stores, party supply stores, children's party
Children's party entertainment •Magician •Musician •Mime •Singer •Storyteller	$50+	Children's clothing stores, toy stores, bookstores, day care centers
Coach (sports)	Varies	Children's clothing stores, sporting goods stores
Dance instruction	$35+/Hr	Dance supply stores, children's clothing stores
Embroidery	Varies	Needlework shops, fabric stores, art supply stores
Flower arranging	Varies	Home decorating stores, florists, craft shops
Handwriting analyst	$35+/session	Bookstores, health clubs, stationery stores
Horseback riding	Varies	Sporting goods stores, health clubs instruction
Image consultant	$35+/session	Clothing stores, hair salons
Knitting	Varies	Needlepoint stores, craft stores
Monogramming	Varies	Needlepoint stores, craft stores, dry cleaners
Needlepoint	Varies	Needlepoint stores, craft stores
Numerologist	$50+/session	Bookstores, New Age stores
Party clown	$50+	Party supply stores, balloon bouquet stores, card shops

Photographer	Varies	Day care centers, stationery supply stores, restaurants
Piano instruction	$40+	Music stores, elementary schools
Quilting	Varies	Craft stores, antique stores
Reweaving	Varies	Dry cleaners, tailor shops
Sewing	Varies	Fabric stores, hair salons, health clubs, dry cleaners
Shopping service	$10+/Hr.	Busy office buildings, health clubs, hair salons
Singing telegram	$50+	Party supply stores, balloon bouquet stores, card shops
Tennis instruction	$35+/Hr.	Health clubs, restaurants, sporting goods stores
T-shirt design	Varies	Sporting goods stores, weight loss centers
Yoga instructor	$20+/Hr.	Health clubs, hair salons, massage centers

MORE IDEAS FOR MAKING MONEY

If you can help someone solve a problem, save time, save money, offer a unique skill, or do an unsavory chore, you can make money. What resources do you have in terms of equipment or know-how? Perhaps your computer or video camera could be used to offer a service. Sometimes the best ideas are right under your nose, but you just haven't thought about turning it into a business. Try to think about your talents in a new way. Here are more ideas for making money:

> "I never thought about my photography as anything more than a hobby until my neighbor asked me to take pictures at her child's birthday party. Now I have fun being around kids on the weekends, and I make $25 an hour as a photographer."—Ron, 26

More Cash-Generating Ideas

Auctioneer
Basement/attic/garage cleaning
Bookkeeping
Caning repair
Car pool service
Carpet cleaning
Ceiling repair
Closet organizing
Copywriter
Desktop publishing
Doll repair
Facialist/skin care instructor
Furniture stripping/repair
Genealogy research service
Gift basket service
Graphic design
Grant writing
Herb growing

Interpreting service
Inventory household effects
Language instruction/tutor
Lawn mower repair
Makeup consultant
Manuscript editing/proofreading
Modeling
People-tracing service
Property maintenance
Rare book finding service
Reupholstering
Roof inspection
Sewing machine repair
Sightseeing guide
Software writer
Speech writer
Venetian blind cleaning
Videotape service

MARKETING, MARKETING, MARKETING

People will buy your service if they hear about, need it, and the price is right. First, they must hear about it. So your task is to devise a marketing plan that really reaches the people who are likely to want or need what you have to offer. It doesn't have to be lengthy or elaborate. In fact, a few well-focused efforts may be all you really need. Many of the following strategies are free or very inexpensive—and they really work:

Newspaper Articles

Many local and community papers accept freelance articles that offer readers interesting information. How-to articles often capture attention and earn you recognition as an authority on the subject. At the end of the article, have your name and service mentioned in a short profile. Some publishers will even agree to barter a small ad space in exchange for your article.

Classified Advertising

Scan your local and community papers for competitors' ads. Choose publications that closely target the readership audience you want to attract for your service.

Send Personal Notes

Personal contact is often one of the most effective methods for soliciting new business. Try offering an introductory half-price special. This works especially well if your service is a regular, repeat business.

Give Speeches

Community groups and nonprofit service organizations are constantly looking for new speakers who live nearby (no travel expenses) and are willing to speak free of charge. Contact the organizations directly by phone. Offer your time for a short instructional talk to their lunch or dinner group in exchange for networking time with their members. You may even be able to get a copy of their membership mailing list. Be sure to bring your fliers to hand out before and after the speech.

Hand Out Business Cards

Everywhere you go, you will run into people who need your service or know someone who might. Always keep a pocket full of cards handy, and don't be shy. Talk it up! It's amazing how small the world is.

Teach Classes

Many local YWCAs offer a regular schedule of non-credit courses on a wide variety of topics. Call the director to offer your skills or talents. If the YWCA doesn't offer them in your area, find out who does, or consider doing it yourself.

Donating Your Service

Charitable and fundraising organizations hold auctions and silent auctions on a regular basis. Hundreds (even thousands) of people view the items and have the opportunity to bid on them. By donating your service, you can gain significant exposure. Oftentimes, the auction organizers will give you a list of the people who bid on your item so that you may follow up with them.

Fax

Business-to-business fax is a '90s way to inform others of your service. As an alternative to delivering fliers, a short phone call with a fact sheet follow-up is often very effective in generating referral business.

Online Networking

Another '90s technique to spreading the word is online, through an online service or directly on the Internet. It's a natural for businesses that can be conducted by mail, such as handwriting analysis or word processing.

Press Releases

Tried and true when it comes to newsworthy events, press releases can be your best promotional strategy. When you have a few happy customers, write about them.

Enlist Your Friends to Make Money for You

Who would like to make money by just talking? Probably almost everyone you know. Create a win-win incentive for your friends to earn a portion of your fee for giving you business referrals.

Networking can be one of the most powerful income generators for any service business. And by enlisting your friends with a financial incentive, you multiply your sales force exponentially.

Establish a few ground rules to reduce the chance of a misunderstanding or confusion. Conflicts about money can quickly cool an otherwise good friendship. Written guidelines discussed beforehand are always a good idea. They may include any of the following suggestions, as appropriate for your situation:

1. What is the fee per referral? ($5? $10?)

2. How is the referral made? Must the customer mention the person who referred him or her?

3. When is the fee paid? (Suggestion: after you collect from the customer.)

4. What if more than one person refers a customer?

5. How are disputes resolved?

In fact, once you have satisfied customers, you can offer them a referral fee for new business. They probably all have lots of friends who could use your service, especially if you have done a good job and your price beats the competition. The miniblind cleaner mentioned earlier gives a free cleaning to any customers who refer new customers and a $20 referral fee to anyone else sending business her way. "I'm thrilled to reward people for sending new business, because it keeps snowballing."

CHAPTER 4

Banking Basics

Think of banking as a relationship—a very important one. Your entire financial life will depend on how well you manage your money. Banks are at the heart of this, and your relationship with your bank will pave the way for your financial success or failure.

> Ginger, 24, tells this horror story about her experience with bad credit: "I made some poor choices that resulted in overextending myself financially. My bad credit haunted me for seven years. It caused unbelievable problems and hassles. I'd never handle credit like that again."

Use your banking relationship as a springboard to earning a favorable credit rating.

Banks are constantly looking for new business, particularly if you are conscientious and intend to build a solid foundation. Your banking relationships are pivotal to proving that you manage your money in a reliable fashion and are worthy of being trusted with additional credit. On the other hand, if you don't really care about how many checks you bounce or how late your payments are, then they probably won't care to have your business, either.

WHAT BANKS OFFER YOU

Here's a quick introduction to the services banks provide.

Savings Accounts

Start here. By all means, if you haven't had a savings account all your life, it's time. Run (don't walk) to the bank of your choice and open your savings account immediately, even if it's only for the minimum acceptable balance. Savings accounts are imperative to send the message that you intend to save money and handle your finances responsibly.

Checking Accounts

The very next building block of your financial future is a basic checking account. Open one today. It enables you to manage money on paper and prove that you are capable. Keep enough money in it to handle the expenses you anticipate during a typical month. Avoid overdrafts and late fees like the plague. They can be reported to the credit bureau and sabotage your chances for obtaining credit.

Money Market Accounts

A money market account combines the benefits of a savings account and a checking account. Just like a savings account, a money market account pays you interest on your money. And much like a checking account, a money market account lets you write checks. But beware! You may have to maintain a minimum balance to avoid a monthly service charge that eats away at your earnings. And the bank may impose minimums on the check amount or a maximum on the number of checks you may write each month—another way to charge fees and decrease your earnings. So get the facts on all fees and service charges before you jump to conclusions about the best type of account for you.

Overdraft Checking

If you have no credit, overdraft privileges are often the first step in establishing your repayment history with a bank. The overdraft extension is actually a line of credit (a debt) that you incur by writing checks for more than the balance in your account. Get the details straight about specific repayment requirements and procedures. Be sure to follow them to the letter in order to establish a favorable track record.

Automated Teller Machines (ATMs)

With your ATM card and personal code number, both issued by the bank, you may make a cash deposit, withdraw cash, or transfer money from one account to another. Each transaction is directly posted to your checking account, and you must record it in your check register immediately. Banks are increasingly charging up to one dollar per transaction, particularly for use of machines located at competitors' institutions.

Debit Cards

Debit cards are used just like checks. Transactions are posted directly to your account. Unlike credit cards, there is no bill at the end of the month. Each transaction acts just like cash, and must be recorded in your check register. And, unlike checks, there is no "float," or lag time, between the time you use the card and the time it takes to "clear" your account. Banks often assess a monthly or annual fee for the debit card.

Additional Bank Products and Services

For your convenience, banks offer a wide array of financial products and services, including:

- Traveler's checks
- Cashier's checks
- Certified checks
- Money orders
- Certificates of deposit (CDs)
- U.S. Government savings bonds
- Mutual funds and annuities
- Trust accounts
- Loans
- Bank cards (such as MasterCard™ and Visa™)
- Safe deposit boxes
- Life insurance
- Retirement plans
- Direct deposit
- Computer banking
- Phone banking
- Joint accounts

SHOP FOR THE RIGHT BANK FOR YOU

You have lots of choices, including commercial banks, savings and loans, credit unions, and even "nonbanks." Here's how they stack up:

Commercial Banks

Often called full-service banks, they originally catered to businesses. Individuals now benefit from their wide range of services.

Pros: • Federal Deposit Insurance Corporation (FDIC) insures deposits up to $100,000

• Well-located branches

Cons: • High fees

• Less personal service

• Less flexible hours

Savings and Loans

Originally catering to individuals' needs for loans, S&Ls have now diversified their product offerings to accommodate a wider range of consumer needs.

Pros: • Lower fees

• More personal service

• Might be open evenings and Saturdays

• Most are federally insured

Cons: • Historically more failures

• Fewer branch locations

Credit Unions

Usually nonprofit cooperative institutions, credit unions serve a group with a similar bond, such as large employers or church groups.

Pros: • Lower fees and service charges

• Earnings are paid out to members at year-end

Cons: • Only 90 percent are federally insured. About 5 percent are privately insured

• Checks are not returned to you. You must keep a carbon copy yourself

Nonbank Banks

Special accounts may be serviced through nonbank entities. For example, brokerage houses now offer check-writing capabilities on money market mutual fund accounts.

Pros: • Might offer high interest, even tax-free interest

Cons: • Range of services are limited

• Not FDIC insured, but might have private insurance

HOW TO DECIDE WHICH KIND OF INSTITUTION TO USE

The choices can seem overwhelming. When you boil it all down, the key factors to evaluate include products and services, costs, convenience, and stability:

Products and Services

❏ Does the institution offer all the products and services you need, or would you have to use two or more institutions?

❏ If you demonstrate your responsible management of cash, would they consider extending you a small line of credit?

Costs

❏ Do they require minimum amounts to open accounts?

❏ Do they require minimum monthly balances to avoid fees or service charges?

❏ What fees or service charges are assessed and why?

❏ Under what conditions are the fees or service charges waived?

❏ Does the account pay interest?

❏ What do checks cost?

❏ What do ATM transactions cost?

❏ How can you keep costs down?

Convenience

❏ Is it close to home, school, or work?

❏ Are the hours conducive to your schedule?

❏ Is the institution constantly busy, with long lines and long waits?

❏ Can you use automated teller machines as an alternative?

Stability

❏ Are they covered up to $100,000 per account by federal insurance (FDIC)?

FEES, FEES, FEES

Banks charge fees like there's no tomorrow. A prominent financial industry newsletter reported that altogether, financial institutions charged more than 225 different fees in 1993. Four years earlier, that total was only 95. And during that time, the amount of each fee increased an average of 15 percent. So watch out! It's your job as a smart consumer to focus on finding the best deal for the lowest fee. Before you open an account, ask your customer service representative to give you fee details on:

❏ Monthly maintenance fees or service charges

❏ Transaction fees or per-check fees

❏ Excessive-transaction fees

❏ Inadequate-balance charges

❏ Bounced-check charges

❑ Stop-payment fees

❑ ATM transaction fees at your bank's machine

❑ ATM transaction fees at another bank's machine

❑ Balance-inquiry charges

❑ Charges for assistance in balancing your account

❑ Overdraft protection fees or interest charges

Banks often lure new customers in with the promise of free checking. It sounds great, but nothing is free. You will pay for it through fees and charges assessed on your accounts and transactions. So before you sign up, read the fine print to find out what they are and how much they'll cost.

Financial aid counselors advise students to ask about special programs and rates for students. "Then come ask us about helping you decide which one meets your needs and offers the best value. We're here to help."

In addition to getting details on fees, you'll want to find out about these services and charges:

What is the minimum balance required to avoid fees?
For interest-earning accounts, what is the:

- Interest rate?
- Minimum balance required to earn interest?
- Compounding method? (Daily? Monthly? Quarterly?)

ATM TIPS

Many people rarely conduct their banking inside the bank—they use an ATM. This is often more convenient during evening and weekend hours when traditional bank lobbies and drive-throughs are closed. If ATMs are part of your lifestyle, be aware of these important tips:

- Keep your Personal Identification Number (PIN) strictly confidential. Allowing someone to use it even once jeopardizes your security.

- Some banks now charge for transactions at their own machines. Most banks charge 50 cents to $1.00 for transactions at another bank's machine.

- Be doubly sure to enter each and every transaction in your check register and keep a running balance. Forgotten ATM withdrawals are a major source of overdrafts.

- Keep all ATM transaction receipts until you balance your account. Make sure that all transactions posted properly.

- Notify the bank within two business days of learning that your card was lost or stolen to limit your liability to $50. After two days, your liability escalates to $500. If you fail to report the loss within 60 days after the statement was mailed, you risk losing all the money in your account plus any unused portion of your overdraft line of credit.

- To be safe, deposit cash only with a personal teller inside the bank lobby.

Using Your Checking Account—Common Questions and Answers

What if I make a mistake while writing a check?
Tear it out and write "VOID" in the space in your check register. Don't just write "VOID" on the check. It could fall into the hands of a forger. Instead, tear the check up completely.

Can I stop payment of a check?
As long as the check has not yet cleared the account, you may call to have them issue a stop-payment order. Most institutions discourage this practice and charge a healthy fee, up to $20 or more. Ask how long the stop payment order is in effect. It may be renewable at the end of that time.

What happens when a check "bounces"?
Generally, the bank assesses a hefty service charge—as high as $30. If you run your balance close to zero, the service charge could cause an even greater overdraft, resulting in more bad checks and more service charges. The bank may or may not call you to notify you of the situation. Ask in advance about their policy on bounced checks.

How can I avoid overdrafts?

It helps to keep close track of each transaction, diligently entering the dates, amounts, and running balance. Reconcile the account every month and keep enough money in the account to give you a little breathing room.

Why should the monthly statement be "balanced"?

Either you or the bank may have made errors. Balancing, or reconciling, your account will show you the difference in the bank's recorded transactions and yours. Reconciling your account is the only way to ensure that your records match.

How is the monthly statement balanced?

Specific instructions are provided on the back of the statement. If you have trouble, ask the customer service representative for help. If it's your first time, you may be able to make an appointment and get assistance for a nominal charge, or none at all.

What are the most common errors causing a bank account not to balance?

Although banks do make mistakes, most of the errors are ours, not the bank's. They include:

- Checks or withdrawals you forgot to enter in your check register
- Checks or withdrawals entered incorrectly
- Errors in addition or subtraction
- Fees charged by the bank and not entered in your check register
- Errors by the bank (such as posting amounts twice)

"Whenever I compare my checkbook figures with my bank statement, I always find my checkbook a few dollars short. But I never thought that it was a big deal until the day my numbers were off by over $200. I thought the bank had messed up so I demanded my money back. But it turned out that I had actually forgotten to record several $20 ATM withdrawals. I felt pretty stupid!"—Sumi, 20

What if the monthly statement has an error?

Notify the bank as soon as you notice the error. Mistakes involving electronic transfers should be resolved within 60 days while others are allowed only 14 days. Save original transaction receipts for proof, and compare them to the monthly statement when it arrives.

How long should I save canceled checks?

Save checks as proof of payment in case of a dispute. For most consumer purchases, that may be only several months to a year. For IRS disputes, you may wish to save these documents for several years.

How does an endorsement protect the check?

If the check is simply endorsed with a signature of the payee, it may be cashed by anyone who possesses it. For protection, the payee places a restriction above the endorsement. For example, "For Deposit Only—Account # xxx-xxxx" is handwritten at the top. Then the payee signs below. With this restriction, the check must be deposited to the specified account. It may not be cashed.

What if my checkbook is lost or stolen?

Notify the bank immediately. They will likely put a hold on the account and monitor each check as it is presented for payment.

$ECTION 2
Debt and Credit

CHAPTER 5

Credit Cards

Americans use over 200 million credit cards. They carry an average debt balance of $1,300 per card. With over 6,000 issuers of credit cards offering a menu of rates, fees, and incentives, your credit choices may seem overwhelming. A wide range of credit card products is available, including bank cards, store cards, debit cards, and travel and entertainment cards.

Some companies, like American Express™ and Discover™, offer cards directly to consumers. Credit associations, like MasterCard and Visa, offer their credit through banks that sign up the consumers. Each type of credit card product is unique, and carries different terms for the consumer.

How Do Credit Cards Work?

Which type of credit card is right for you? How can you get the best rates and terms? Demystifying this maze of confusion is really not so tough. First, take a look at how credit cards work. All of them really have a common underlying process:

1. When you make a purchase on your MasterCard, for instance, the store checks the validity of the card and your available credit balance by running your card through its electronic approval machine. Your signed receipt is essentially your contract agreement to pay for the purchase.

2. The store sends all receipts to MasterCard within five days. MasterCard acts as the clearinghouse.

3. MasterCard sends notice to the store's bank; the store's bank pays the store the total amount of receipts minus a 2.7% service fee.

4. MasterCard charges the bank that issued you the card the same amount. Your bank then pays the store's bank.

5. Your bank sends you a statement, requesting payment from you.

In this example, banks are involved. For store cards and travel and entertainment cards, the credit is supplied directly by the company. Here are some other distinguishing features of the different types of credit cards.

Store Cards
Examples: Department stores such as Sears and J.C. Penney. Oil companies such as Exxon and Shell.
These are really charge cards, enabling you to charge purchases only at that company's stores. A minimum monthly payment is required each month, or the balance may be paid in full. Any unpaid balance accrues interest. Generally, interest rates are very high, but there is no annual fee.

Bank Cards
Examples: Visa, MasterCard, Optima™, and Discover.
These are issued by bank members under a licensing agreement with the organization. Under the agreement, each issuing bank member must honor the drafts of thousands of retail member organizations all over the world. Since credit card products can be quite profitable, the competition is fierce. A minimum monthly payment is required each month. You can shop around to get favorable rates and incentives. An annual fee may or may not be assessed.

Travel and Entertainment Cards
Examples: American Express, Diner's Club™, and Carte Blanche™
All purchases must be paid in full at the end of each month. You also pay an annual fee (usually $50–$75), but you pay no interest.

Debit Cards
These may look like credit cards, but any charges that you make are immediately deducted from your bank account. Using a debit card is really more like writing a check than using a charge card. You have no "credit," and you cannot spend more than the balance in your account.

HOW TO APPLY FOR A CREDIT CARD

If you're just starting out, store cards may be easier to get than bank cards or travel and entertainment cards. They're eager to get your retail business, so if you have good bank references from your checking and savings account, you have a good shot at getting at least a small line of credit at their store. Credit counselors agree, although they caution beginners to use good judgment. "Just because credit cards are available, they're not for everyone. Only people who can pay the bill at the end of the month should apply for cards and use them." After using a small credit line, you can usually increase the amount after making timely payments and handling the account prudently for six to twelve months. Here are some more tips for successfully applying for credit cards.

- Begin by requesting and studying your credit report (see the chapter called "Take Charge of Your Credit Report"). Find out what your credit report says about you before your prospective creditors do. Fix any errors or problems right away. Do not send out credit applications before you have proof that the errors are corrected to your satisfaction.

- Calculate your personal debt-to-income ratio. Add all of your monthly expenses. Divide this total by your monthly income (see the section called "Take Inventory of Your Debt and Monthly Payments" in chapter 8). To be considered a good risk by most creditors, your ratio should be less than 40 percent.

- Apply to one company at a time. If you are rejected, find out precisely why you were rejected. If it is a problem you can rectify, do so before you apply to another company.

- Watch newspaper ads for special promotions by banks and financial institutions. Since competition is so strong, consumers may benefit by special offers on rates and terms.

- Mid-size regional banks often offer the best rates.

- Ask the company what their credit requirements are. Before you officially apply, you can make a fairly accurate assessment of your chances for approval under their guidelines.

- Fill out the application in detail, neatly and accurately. Remember, first impressions count.

- Always include full information about your checking and savings accounts. If you don't have a checking account and a savings accounts, open them immediately.

WHAT DOES CREDIT COST?

Credit doesn't have to cost an arm and a leg. But it might. Consider this: If you pay your balance in full at the end of each billing cycle, your interest charges may be zero. And if you have a card with no annual fee, you pay virtually nothing for the use of their money for up to 30 days.

Credit card companies build a highly profitable business around customers who don't pay their balance in full. In fact, the amount carried forward each month generally grows as customers pay only a small minimum balance and charge even more next month. This is how millions of Americans find themselves in an often hopeless cycle of debt. "I got into a nightmare situation with credit cards. It's so easy to charge and you don't realize that the minimum monthly payment doesn't come close to paying down your debt," reports a college student who had to get a job just to pay off his credit cards. Escalating debt and interest charges could keep you in financial bondage if you're not smart about managing your credit use. Here's a simple example of how expensive debt can be:

> You charge $1,000 on your credit card. The interest rate is 16.5 percent and the minimum payment is 2.5 percent of the outstanding balance. If you make only the minimum payment each month, it will take you eight years and eight months to pay the card off completely. The total of all your payments will amount to $1,766. However, if you paid the minimum balance plus $10 each month, you would pay $500 less in interest and pay the card off in three years.

Now, think about how this problem is compounded when you make additional charges every month, increasing the total debt, but making only the minimum payment. You can quickly create a financial sinkhole. But you don't have to. The solution is simple; pay the entire balance in full at the end of each billing cycle. You will pay no interest and accumulate no debt. Credit counselors agree, "Paying the full amount off each month is extremely important. If you let a balance accumulate, it will snowball and keep you in debt."

How Finance Charges Are Calculated

As a smart consumer, it's important to know how the finance charge is calculated. Three methods are generally used, and each one affects how much interest you pay on the balance you carry.

Adjusted Balance Method: This is the least expensive method. Your payment is subtracted from the beginning balance and interest is charged on the remainder. No interest is charged on purchases during the billing period.

Average Daily Balance Method: This is the most common method. Interest is charged on the average of the amount you owe each day during the period. So, the larger your payment, the lower your interest charge.

Previous Balance Method: This is the most expensive method. Interest is charged on the total amount you owe at the beginning of the period.

The amount of interest you pay each month varies widely depending on which of these methods is employed. For example, assume you have a beginning balance of $2,000 on your card. Suppose you make a payment of $1,000 on the 15th (halfway through the billing cycle). If your creditor charges 18 percent annual interest (or 1.5 percent per month), the interest charge under each method would be:

Adjusted Balance Method:	$15.00
Average Daily Balance Method:	$22.50
Previous Balance Method:	$30.00

Credit Card Terms

With so many different types of cards and so much competition for your business, there is no standard for terms and charges. In fact, companies are getting so creative with their programs and pricing that it's often very difficult for the consumers to know just what they're being charged. It's quite complicated, and most cards are different. So, if you do carry an outstanding balance from one month to the next, it is wise to empower yourself by doing a bit of research.

Each creditor is required to give you specific information on terms when you sign on for a card. But most of us don't take time to read the fine print. Even when we do, it tends to be so complicated and technical that it's of little use. If you really want to nail this information down, use the following checklist:

❏ How much is the annual fee (if any)?

❏ What is the stated interest rate?

❏ If the interest rate is variable, when does it change? By how much?

❏ If the interest rate is tiered, when does it change? By how much?

❏ Is the interest rate based on average daily balances?

❏ If so, do the average daily balances include or exclude new purchases?

❏ Is there a grace period for payments?

❏ If so, when does it begin?

What fees are charged for:

    ❏ Each transaction?

    ❏ Late payments?

    ❏ Cash advances?

    ❏ Exceeding the credit limit?

    ❏ ATM use?

❏ What other fees are charged?

BILLING ERRORS AND PROBLEMS

Be sure to review your monthly statement. Pay special attention to the charges, verifying that you made them. "I like to keep my charge slips in my wallet. Then at the end of the month, I compare them to the statement to make sure that they are all correct," advises one beginner who handles her cards wisely. Mistakes do happen.

You have rights under the Fair Credit Billing Act in the event of billing errors and/or problems, including:

- Defective merchandise
- Wrong goods or services
- Incorrect payments or credits
- Disputed charges or amounts
- Computational errors
- Other errors or problems

The law provides that you have 60 days from the statement date to notify the creditor in writing of the exact nature of the dispute. In turn, they have 30 days to respond and 90 days to resolve the problem. In the meantime, they cannot restrict you from using your card, and they cannot release poor credit information on you during the dispute. To see what a typical billing problem dispute letter looks like, check out the sample at the end of this chapter.

Other tips to expedite or avoid credit disputes:

- Keep copies of all correspondence about your credit.

- Keep notes of all phone conversations, including name, date, time, topics discussed, and actions agreed upon by each individual.

- You may also add up to 100 words to your credit report to explain the extenuating circumstances of a negative item in your report. For more information on amending your credit report, see the chapter called "Take Charge of Your Credit Report."

Protect Yourself from Credit Card Fraud

Credit card fraud is big business. According to spokespeople at major bank card companies, one out of 5,000 cards is subject to some type of fraud. Counterfeiting abounds; all that's needed is a valid account number. Technology has made fraud easy and relatively inexpensive. Even though consumer protection legislation protects you from fraudulent charges in excess of $50, straightening the mess out is a colossal headache and major waste of your time. You can take significant measures to protect your credit:

- Sign the back of each card as soon as you receive it.

- Never sign a blank charge slip (this is a common practice for deposits!)

- Always keep your credit card receipts to verify the charges on your statement.

- Always tear up the carbons when you use your card.

- Do not give your credit card number out for identification on the back of your check.

- Avoid giving your card number out over the phone.

- Keep a list of your account numbers and the company's customer service number so you'll know whom to call if your cards are ever lost or stolen.

COMMONLY ASKED QUESTIONS

How many credit cards are enough?

Generally, a few well-handled credit cards will serve you well as you establish a track record. No more than six, preferably only three. Creditors do not want to see an extensive list of available credit cards, because with lots of available credit, you could charge them all up and get into trouble.

Are cards that give frequent flier miles a good deal?

Yes, so long as you're not paying interest, any freebie is great. If you're carrying a monthly balance and paying interest, watch out. The rate should be comparable to similar cards without giveaways, or you may be paying for the giveaway through a higher rate.

How can I find the best credit card deals?

Use the credit card checklist from this chapter to compare the terms. But remember, your objective is to be a wise consumer by carrying no balance and eliminating all credit card–related expenses.

Should I use my credit card number on the Internet?

Many people do, just as they use it over the phone. As with any confidential financial information, you are at greater risk of fraud when you disclose your credit card account number and authorize use from a remote location. To be safer, don't do it.

When is it time to cut up my credit cards?

When you feel out of control, or when you can't make the monthly payments. Stop charging before you dig yourself in deeper. And seek professional guidance.

Billing Problem Dispute Letter

Date

Name of Creditor
Name of Credit Manager
Street Address
City, State, Zip

Dear (Name of Credit Manager),

Regarding my account (account #) the following item is incorrect on my statement dated (date):

(Give details of the error or problem, including specifically what you believe the appropriate resolution should be.)

Please research and correct the problem. Mail your response to me at the address below.

In the meantime, I am withholding payment for the amount of this dispute ($ amount). Do not report this amount as a late payment or release negative credit information, in accordance with the Fair Credit Billing Act.

Sincerely,

Your name as it appears on the account
Your account number
Your address
Your phone number

CHAPTER 6

How to Establish (Good) Credit

Have you ever tried to rent a truck to move? Or make hotel reservations? Or pay for your purchases with a check? If so, chances are you've been asked for a credit card. Not because you're charging it, but because you need to produce some plastic before they'll take your check, or rent you the hotel room, or the truck. Not having good credit can be frustrating, making it much harder for you to live in this credit-oriented world.

> "I couldn't believe how hard it is to rent a truck without a credit card. Since I don't have one, I had to get my friend to rent the truck for me." —Stuart, 20.

Did you know that if you apply for a job with an annual salary of $20,000 or more, your potential employer could obtain a copy of your credit report without your knowledge or permission? Your credit rating might be a very valuable asset or a very real barrier to success. Landlords have every right to request a copy of your credit report at any time. When you apply for an apartment, you might very well be competing for it on the basis of your credit rating. Aaron, 21, was disappointed to find out that he had lost out on a great apartment near his new job just because another applicant had a better credit rating. "It really upset me. I applied first and offered a deposit check on the spot. The landlady wouldn't take it before she ran a credit check. I really wanted that apartment. Now I have to drive across town to get to work."

Credit is a way of life in America today. We are constantly ambushed with solicitations to incur debt, through the mail, newspaper, television, radio, magazines, billboards, and even our monthly bills and bank statements. Finance companies, retailers, banks, auto dealers, and credit card companies all feverishly urge us to spend more money than we have. They promote what appear to be unbelievably good deals (really unbelievable!) on auto loans, bill consolidation loans, credit cards, holiday loans, cash advances, and home improvement loans, among other extremely creative and tempting offers. No wonder we have problems with overspending. Consumers are taking advantage of these financial products with some pretty scary results.

According to the United States Department of Commerce, American credit card debt was $80.2 billion in 1980. By 1991, that amount had increased 322 percent to $257.9 billion! Our society is very quickly becoming a society of people who use credit as a way of life. And credit use easily slides into credit misuse and credit abuse. Don't let that happen to you. Your challenge is to obtain and use your credit wisely, so that it helps instead of hurts you.

How Are Credit and Debt Different?

Although credit card debt was $257.9 billion in 1991, spending by credit cards was $481 billion. Only $223.1 billion, or 46 percent of all credit card purchases, were paid off. The rest of the spending turned into burdensome debt. If you join the average American in this escalating pattern of credit card abuse, you will fall into a serious debt spiral. Guaranteed.

Over one billion credit cards are in circulation in America today. The average consumer carries at least six credit cards. They have a ready ability to use credit, but any given individual (including you) does not have to be in debt. This distinction is important for you to understand, especially as it relates to your own ability to obtain credit, while applying your good judgment in using the credit you have and avoiding debt. The solution may be summed up in three basic steps:

1. Establish good credit.

2. Use your credit (yes, charge purchases occasionally), but always pay the balance in full each billing cycle. Never "carry" a balance over to the next billing cycle.

3. Do not spend more than you can pay off completely at the end of the billing cycle.

Follow these simple rules and you'll be rewarded with a lifetime of financial opportunity in the world of credit. You'll beat the traps of abusive spending and debting that millions of Americans find themselves caught in and struggling to survive year after year.

Steps to Establishing Good Credit

Since every creditor has different lending guidelines and every consumer has a unique situation, no standard, sure-fire formula exists to ensure that you will qualify for credit. But you can greatly improve your chances of getting approved and establishing a very favorable track record that works for you.

- Start now, even if you're still in school.
- Maintain steady employment.
- Join the credit union where you work (or wherever you're eligible).
- Open checking and savings accounts.
- Apply for credit at your bank.
- Apply for a secured credit card.
- Apply for credit cards at a department store or service station.
- Pay all charges off in full each billing cycle.
- Request and study copies of your credit report periodically.

Start Now, Even If You're Still in School

Ironically, college students often have an easier time obtaining first-time credit than young people with full-time jobs. Credit card issuers believe that college students will become college graduates who will eventually earn more, buy more, and charge more than their less-educated counterparts. They want to capture this buying loyalty early. One credit card executive agrees, "We target the college student population pretty heavily. We believe that they're a bright, young group who handle their responsibilities well, and their credit will grow as they graduate and land lucrative jobs." And, of course, many students have parents who will co-sign their debt and/or pay it off if they get into trouble. As credit risks go, college students are not a bad bet. The default rate for college students is statistically no different than that of the average American consumer—four to five percent.

Maintain Steady Employment

Rule of thumb: Any employment is better than no employment. Even unskilled labor at a part-time job will give you a higher rating than none at all. To improve your rating, stay at your job for a respectable period of time. The longer you stay, the more stable you'll appear to potential creditors.

Join a Credit Union

Credit unions may well be the least understood and most underutilized type of credit facility in America today. They offer a wide array of financial products, often at very favorable rates and terms. When you maintain a savings account with your credit union, they are inclined to grant credit quite easily for a variety of uses. For example, 75 percent of all credit unions offer members credit cards, with interest rates averaging 4 percent lower than national bank card companies.

But because you must be a member of a credit union to use their services, many people are not aware of the benefits and do not realize that they are eligible to join one. Only half of all eligible adults are actually members of credit unions. And up to 70 percent of all adults are eligible. To find out if you qualify for membership in any credit union, call the Credit Union National Association at (800) 356-9655.

Open Checking and Savings Accounts

Your banking relationship is integral to establishing new credit. By managing your account in a responsible and conscientious manner, you are paving the way for creditors to begin to trust you with more risk. So do everything in your power to avoid overdrafts due to insufficient balances, late payments, and penalties. Maintain minimum balances as required. Find out specifically what they report to the credit bureaus and when. All banks have policies for reporting credit activity. When you open your account, find out what their credit reporting policies are. Then make sure you stick to their guidelines to ensure that their reports on you are favorable.

Apply for Credit at Your Bank

After you prove that you are handling the basic checking and savings accounts to their satisfaction, the bank will be more inclined to begin to grant you real credit. This often comes in the way of overdraft privileges on your checking account. Be careful. Handle this privilege with kid gloves. Do not spend more money than you have. Use the overdraft allowance exclusively for the purpose of establishing your good credit. If you feel you cannot restrain yourself, then don't use this technique.

> "My checkbook balance was never accurate. I had an overdraft line, but it only caused me to go into debt. I had to close it in order to get straightened out. I guess I'm not ready to deal with this, yet," admitted Marla, 20.

The only financially responsible reason to draw on your overdraft line is to establish credit, not to spend money that you really don't have.

When you use this method, start with an amount that is significant enough to establish your creditworthiness (perhaps half of the approved overdraft amount, maximum), but not so much that it could cause you a financial burden (perhaps one day's pay, minimum). The right amount for you will be an amount you feel comfortable with and have confidence that you can handle easily. Do not spend the money you draw. Ever. Put it in your savings account or safe deposit box. Then repay the overdraft within a very short period of time. You'll have to pay interest on the amount you draw on your overdraft line. Consider it one of the costs of establishing good credit.

Apply for a Secured Credit Card

A fairly easy way to begin to establish credit with a bank is through a secured credit card. You are granted a line of credit on your card, but you must maintain a specified balance in your savings account. The outstanding balance may not exceed the amount in savings. This method is generally more expensive because the interest rate on the card is higher. And you are tying up a specific balance in your savings as collateral for the repayment of your credit card debt. But it is an effective method to get you started when others don't work.

Use a secured card for a year or so. Then when you have a good track record on timely payments, you may apply for unsecured cards. Chances are, you'll be approved for new credit once you've proven yourself with a secured card first. The same rules for paying off the balance in full are important to abide by here, too. Don't consider your savings a source of repayment. Consider your savings to be untouchable. Always.

Apply for Credit Cards at a Department Store or Service Station

Service station cards may be easier to get, but most don't report to credit bureaus. They are virtually useless as sources of good credit reports. However, you may find that if you have some credit cards, others will be easier to get. By obtaining at least one, you may find that department stores will be more inclined to issue you one of theirs.

Remember, these are not to be used to buy things you don't have the cash to pay for or things you wouldn't buy anyway. Use them with the utmost discretion. Pay the bill in full each billing cycle. And remember, you don't have to use them every month. Periodic use for a very limited time will serve your purpose in establishing your good credit rating.

Pay Off all Charges In Full Each Billing Cycle

Credit cards can trap you. It's easy to get trapped, and that's how card companies make money. They allow you to charge today and make a minimum payment (as little as five percent) at the end of the billing cycle. The balance (up to 95 percent of your charge) is carried forward to the next billing cycle. You are charged 18 percent interest or more, being swept into a downward spiral of increasing debt. If you continue to charge more and pay only minimum balances, your debt increases along with your monthly payments.

Many millions of Americans find that they have a tough time paying even the minimum payments, with very little hope of ever paying the balances in full. As you establish credit, you do not have to establish debt. By paying your balance off completely, you are avoiding the trap and building your good credit rating. Good credit enhances your options and choices in life, while carrying debt limits your choices and burdens your financial future.

Credit counselors advise, "The simplest solution is to write a check directly to the credit card company each and every time you charge. Write the check for the full amount of the charge, and subtract it from your checking account balance. Collect all the checks in one place (perhaps a section of your wallet or checkbook). When the monthly statement comes, you should have the total amount outstanding in the form of checks to the credit card company. Just send them in full payment of your bill." This way you have truly adhered to the principle of using your credit in place of cash.

Request and Study Copies of Your Credit Report Periodically

As discussed in detail in the chapter called "Take Charge of Your Credit Report," up to 50 percent of all credit reports contain errors. And they're usually not errors in your favor. Unfortunately, it's up to you to identify and correct these errors in order to assure favorable credit ratings by potential creditors. It's not hard to do, but it will require your time to write a few letters. The procedure is outlined for you in the chapter on credit reports.

TIPS FOR STAYING OUT OF TROUBLE

- Know the difference between being able to charge it and being able to afford it.

- Remember that every time you use a credit card, you are essentially spending cash.

- Keep a log of your charges.

- Write a check to the credit card company each time you charge. Hold all the checks until your bill comes.

- Too many credit applications is a negative on your credit report.

- Never pay late. Never.

- Pay the entire balance off at the end of the billing cycle. Always.

- Do not apply for another card when you've reached your credit limit on the one you're using.

- Having your name on your parents' credit card does not enhance your credit rating, even if you pay all the bills yourself. Any transactions are reported only on your parents' credit report, not yours.

CHAPTER 7

Are You Addicted to Spending?

We all have our little compulsions. Consider the lure of chocolate, the thrill of a bargain, or the rush of coffee in the morning. Or is it the fast food drive-through at midnight? Exercising every day? Just a few more beers? New clothes for your date this weekend?

We don't want to give up such pleasures. And often, we don't have to. Not unless they become uncontrollable, or cause problems in our lives. Chocolate isn't a bad thing. Neither is a bargain. Little pleasures are great in moderation. When they get out of hand through overuse, you might have a problem. That's when addictive behavior begins to set in.

We use compulsions to help us feel better. However, the feeling usually lasts only momentarily, and we have to turn to it again and again to get that feeling back. Since it doesn't really address the cause of our bad feelings, it never solves the underlying problem, and we've found only a quick fix. A recent study looked at the reasons over 1,600 people used little fixes:

- To get extra energy
- To feel a "rush"
- To substitute good feelings for bad feelings
- To fill an empty place inside
- To block upsetting feelings in order to appear cheerful
- To displace anger or frustration
- To patch big problems when they are too busy or tired

HOW SUSCEPTIBLE ARE YOU TO A QUICK FIX?

Fixes offer us a deceptive solution to meeting the nearly impossible demands that society places on us in every aspect of our lives. Not only should we go to the best school, but we are also expected to earn the best grades, land the best job after graduation, have the most fabulous social life, be in top shape athletically, look great at the beach, have this season's way-cool wardrobe, drive the best car, and on and on.

Maybe some people can do it all. For most, it's tough to do without some help from little fixes. Research indicates that reliance on fixes appears to be related to the personality characteristics of people who run at a fast pace. Test yourself to see how you stack up. Take the "Quick Fix Personality Quiz" below.

QUICK FIX PERSONALITY QUIZ

For each of the following, score yourself:

> Never true = 0 points
> Sometimes true = 1 point
> Always true = 2 points

_____ 1. When someone approaches me with a problem, I immediately get involved, even if it's not my responsibility.

_____ 2. I usually do more than my share.

_____ 3. I am very impatient when I have to wait for something.

_____ 4. I am usually harder on myself than other people are on me.

_____ 5. I spend a lot of energy trying to make other people feel better.

_____ 6. My schedule is usually packed, with very little free time.

_____ 7. When I have free time, I usually don't know how to relax.

_____ 8. I try to do things exactly how I like to do them.

_____ 9. I feel that most people don't do things as well as I do.

_____ 10. When I'm on the phone, I like to be doing something else, too, like opening the mail.

_____ 11. I feel guilty when I haven't accomplished everything at the end of the day.

_____ 12. I drive very fast, cutting in and out of lanes to gain position on other cars.

_____ 13. I eat on the fly, never giving too much thought to nutrition.

_____ 14. My family and friends complain that I never have enough time to talk to them.

Now, add up the total points and divide by two. If the result is:

0–3 points: Congratulations! You are not likely to need fixes.

4–7 points: You are having trouble keeping up with your busy self. Watch out!

8–10 points: You are putting undue demands on yourself (and possibly others).

11–14 points: You are in the high risk category and are most likely to use quick fixes.

CAN'T STOP SHOPPING

Although hard statistics are difficult to come by, professional estimates of compulsive shoppers number in the millions. One study suggests that an astounding 27 percent of all women use shopping as a fix. The majority of shopping addicts are women, but a tremendous number of men also shop compulsively. The trouble is, very few of them recognize the problem because our society encourages consumerism.

"My mom and I used to shop together for fun at least twice a week. When I got to college, I suddenly missed it. I was horrified to realize that I was, well, addicted." —Terry, 18

We've grown up in a mad rush to have the best, newest, most expensive, and most sophisticated consumer goods available. Buying has become a national pastime. American consumers are bombarded with over 14,000 advertising messages each and every day. Advertisers and their ad agencies spend billions to get their product message in front of you and make it appear as enticing as humanly possible. They want you to believe that their product will make you happier, more attractive, more successful, more fun, and even more lovable.

Now add the compelling allure of semiannual half-price sales, warehouse clearance events, bargain basements, factory direct outlets, mail order catalogs, and television shopping channels, to name only a few. Tantalizing as they are, most people develop a resistance to the mounting pressure of excessive consumerism. Yet for others, it is not so easy to dismiss. Shopping is a compulsion, and may not be controllable.

THE TOP TEN SIGNS YOU'RE A SHOPAHOLIC

Do you simply enjoy shopping occasionally when you need something? Are you able to manage your shopping budget with little or no effort? Or do you find yourself spending way more than you should on stuff you don't need and can't really afford? If you suspect it might be a problem, be honest with yourself:

❏   1. Do you head to the store when you feel bad and want to get your mind off your problems?

❏   2. Do you ever argue with family or friends about your spending habits?

❏   3. Do you buy things with credit cards that you might not buy with cash?

❏   4. Do you feel a mix of euphoria and anxiety when you shop?

❏   5. Do you feel like you've done something reckless or forbidden when you shop?

❏   6. Do you feel guilty, embarrassed, or confused afterward?

❏   7. Do you lie to family or friends about your purchases?

❏   8. Do you buy things you don't need and never use?

❑ 9. Do you feel lost without your credit cards?

❑ 10. Do you worry about money, but go shopping anyway?

Compulsive shoppers are likely to come home with items that enhance their appearance and their self-image. Clothing, jewelry, makeup, and hair products all promise to boost the ego. But it's a destructive cycle. Shopaholics often live with an underlying sense of anxiety that stems from feelings of inadequacy. "If only I had that new look, I'd attract more dates." Their closets may be a metaphor for their life—internal chaos. They find a temporary release from those feelings through shopping excursions. But once home, the unsettling feelings of confusion and guilt take over and the reality of the negative financial drain sets in. They wind up feeling worse than before. Continually lured by the vague notion of attaining something that's missing, they repeat the cycle.

BREAK THE SHOPPING CYCLE

Begin by asking yourself how you feel when you have an overwhelming desire to shop, and what needs are underneath those feelings. Why do you turn to shopping? Undoubtedly, it's related to your desire for self-esteem, self-worth, and self-renewal. Take the following steps toward freedom:

Acknowledge the problem. Admit to yourself and a safe, trusted friend that it is a problem. Discuss the problem and how it manifests itself in your actions. Discuss your feelings related to your actions. This require courage and self-respect. You can do it.

Take steps to eliminate compulsive behaviors. For instance, if you can't resist stopping at the mall on your way home, then plan another route that bypasses the mall. Two or three behaviors likely put you in the most tempting situations. Identify and eliminate them immediately.

Focus on the underlying needs. Since the shopping is just a fix to compensate for an underlying need, concentrate on defining those needs and meeting them. When you've taken care of that, you'll find that you won't look for a fix anymore.

Forgive yourself. Accept yourself just as you are, defects and all. Ask your trusted friend to accept you just as you are. Remember, we all have flaws (just as we all have gifts). Now concentrate on making a list of your gifts, and love yourself for them.

Reward yourself. *But not by shopping.* Find a reward that's a real treat, like a professional massage, fresh cut flowers at your bedside, a relaxing evening in a hot tub, or a trip to the ocean.

If your addiction is so far out of control that you can't break the habit yourself, Debtors Anonymous offers 145 groups around the country for support and counseling. Compulsive shoppers find that they're not alone and learn about new tools to deal with their spending. The group encourages members to use diaries to record moods and shopping expeditions. Members also develop a strong support network and call experienced members when they have spending urges.

SPORTS GAMBLING ON CAMPUS

Sports gambling has been touted as the "dirty little secret of college life," invisibly growing and thriving on every college campus in America today. Gambling on campus is said to have reached epidemic proportions. And it is far from harmless recreation.

One gambling researcher, Henry Lesieur, Chair of the Criminal Justice Department at Illinois State University, headed a 1991 panel that studied gambling among college students. Their survey of six schools in five states, the largest such study known to date, found that 23 percent of the students gambled at least once a week. Lesieur claims that roughly 5.5 percent of all American college students are pathological gamblers.

At first, the student's attraction starts with betting a few bucks on the game. After all, *everyone does it.* A 1989 Gallup poll reported that 81 percent of the U.S. population gamble. At college, you go to the games with your friends, wear the team colors, cheer the team on, and follow the players' careers. Why not make it a little more interesting? Bets are only $25. By the way, it's fun and profitable, too. No one gets hurt (not yet).

Soon you start betting on other schools in your division. The game is no longer the focal point. It's the money. It's the adrenaline rush from the anticipation and the winning bets. "I loved the pure thrill of winning. But it was depressing to lose. Still, I'd keep going for the win," admits one seasoned sports gambler at a midwestern school. And most compulsive gamblers start out winning. They get a taste for the elusive get-rich-quick dream and can't give up that hope. Many college students find that gambling is immensely easy to get into, because bookies don't ask for cash up front. Everyone who places a bet runs a tab. If you win, you collect. If you lose, you pay up plus 10 percent commission for the bookie. At first, it doesn't sink in that this is real money and real debt.

Soon, the $25 bet becomes two $25 bets. Then more. Many more. It happens fast and spins wildly out of control, although the bettor may not realize it. Once gambling begins, the social environment on many campuses provides pressure to keep it going. Sports-obsessed fans, often in the community of an organization (such as a fraternity house), fueled by weekend parties and alcohol-induced confidence, are often lulled by a mistaken sense of security.

Gambling's Desperate Consequences

Soon the bets escalate to $50 or $100 each, placed on 20 or more games each weekend. One losing weekend can mean financial ruin. Students often run through their financial aid money, run credit cards to the max, and borrow money from relatives to pay off gambling debts. Then they go out and gamble more to repay their loans. If they're on a losing streak, the emotional high becomes emotional devastation, with desperate consequences.

In 1992, a total of $89,000 was stolen from eight Las Vegas banks by a student at the University of Nevada. He robbed the banks to pay off gambling debts. He is currently in Colorado serving a ten-year prison sentence. Similar stories abound.

The Odds Are Against Winning

The intrigue of sports gambling, especially on campus, has been fueled by the media's broadcast of sporting events and related statistics in recent years. ESPN, CNN Headline News' sports ticker, the Internet, satellite dishes, and published injury reports all add to the incredible volume of sports information that's available everywhere, anytime. But most of this information is already absorbed by the odds makers. It's already built into the points spread. Watching a few televised sports shows will not give enough information to beat the odds. Period. Professional handicappers spend twelve hours a day studying sports information and they win only 60 percent of the time.

In addition to the information and points spread disadvantage, the bookmaking operation itself is structured to win in the long run. Few gamblers stop to consider that the 10 percent vigorish (commission) the bookie makes on losing bets will eat away at the bettor's earnings, and will ensure that the bookie profits over time. Sports gambling is designed as a zero-sum game.

THE REAL FIX FOR THE MONEY ADDICT

Behavioral addictions, such as compulsive shopping and gambling, suggest that other problems are at the core. The behavior is only a coping mechanism or smoke screen. Real solutions are found when these issues are addressed:

Perfectionism
Unrealistic expectations of yourself or your performance may lead to feelings of inadequacy and self-deprecation. Ease up on yourself. You'll discover that you don't need to escape through compulsive behaviors.

Control
Are you afraid of most things and feel an overwhelming desire to control the world? Addictive behaviors often present an opportunity for freedom from this anxiety.

Dependency
Dependent personalities often find an illusion of power and prestige in the addictive behavior. It becomes an arena in which they feel empowered.

Loneliness
Isolation breeds compulsive behavior. Each of us needs companionship, just as we need food, clothing, and shelter.

Deception
Addictive behavior is a screen for the real problem within. By engaging in the addictive activity, one can avoid or deny the real problem. This hurts family and friends as the deception grows out of control.

Spirituality
When you feel good about yourself, you are unlikely to resort to compulsive and addictive behaviors. Find your internal center and don't lose it!

CHAPTER **8**

How to Determine
If You're in Trouble

If you suspect that you're overburdened by money problems, *you probably are.* But if you're not sure, then check yourself for these warning signs. If you identify with several of them, it's an indication that trouble may be brewing. If you identify with many or most of them, you are likely headed toward much bigger money problems and would do yourself a major favor by paying attention now. Go ahead and place a check mark next to the items that apply to you.

Typical Warning Signs

❑ You live from paycheck to paycheck.

❑ Your adrenaline starts pumping in the department store. It's a real thrill to spend money.

❑ You find yourself frequently borrowing small amounts of cash from friends.

❑ You wish someone else would handle your finances.

❑ You've paid late charges on credit cards or debts.

❑ You charge what you need because you don't have the cash right now.

❑ You find out how much money is in your checking account by pulling up your balance at the ATM machine.

❑ You rarely balance your bank account.

❑ You know what past due notices look like.

❑ You've received at least one call from a collection agency.

❑ You periodically avoid opening the mail.

❑ You're proud of yourself when you manage to pay the minimum due each month.

❑ You rarely pay more than the minimum due each month.

❑ You get cash advances on credit cards to pay your bills.

❑ You start charging on another credit card when you hit the limit on the one you've been using.

❑ You charge things you want and put off figuring out how you're going to pay for it.

❑ You rarely put money in savings.

❑ You frequently dip into savings to pay bills.

❑ You skip a payment because you can't afford it this month.

❑ Your credit has been canceled for paying your bills late or not at all.

❑ You spend money on entertainment or fun things and can't pay all your bills.

❑ You always get more bills than you expected.

❑ You're caught by surprise when a big bill arrives.

❑ You postdate checks because you won't have the money in your account until later.

❑ You don't know the exact total of all your debt.

❑ You don't know exactly how long it will take to pay off your debt.

❑ You think that someone else will pay your debt off for you.

❑ You're troubled by your finances, but you know that someone will rescue you.

❑ You have a difficult time discussing money.

How did you rate? Did any of these signs ring true? Did you become a bit uncomfortable by the time you finished the list? You'll definitely need to take inventory of your debt and monthly payments and learn how to measure healthy debt (see the section called "Take Inventory of Your Debt and Monthly Payments" in this chapter). Or did you find yourself saying, "It's not really so bad. I can handle it." If this was your reaction, then you may be in denial. Forge on to find out how to deal with it.

DEALING WITH YOUR OWN DENIAL

de.ni.al \ n \ (1): Refusal to admit the truth or reality (2): Assertion that the opposite is true

You say to yourself, "Money is not such a big problem. It's just that I had to spend extra this month (or this week or this year) because of the flat tire (or the birthday present, or the speeding ticket, or the trip to Chicago). I can charge it (or delay paying my bills or get cash from my credit card) until I have the money in the bank. Then I'll catch up." Does this sound familiar? If it takes courage to admit it, then take a harder look. You may be in denial if you find yourself thinking:

• Everyone has too much debt. So what?
• I'm just no good with numbers.
• I can't be expected to deal with this. I was never taught this stuff.
• I'm too young to have to worry about money.
• I'll pay off my bills after I graduate/get a job/get a raise/get a better job.
• But I *have* to spend this money.

Or perhaps you find yourself blaming others or blaming your circumstances. Do you often feel angry because your parents aren't giving you enough money? Do you feel cheated out of money that *should* be yours? Do you resent your boss for not giving you a raise? Do you blame the job market for low pay and unfulfilling work? Are you mad at the department store when your bills are due?

If you've had any of these feelings, *you may be in denial*. And sometimes, denial is a wonderful thing! But if you're feeling pressured, anxious, or depressed about money, then denial isn't working for you anymore. Take heart. There is a way out.

> "I finally couldn't avoid it anymore when I started having bad dreams. I was cranky all day from not sleeping well, and couldn't concentrate at work. It scared me." —Nelson, 23

If nothing changes, nothing changes.

That is, if you continue to do what you're doing, the problem will also continue. Hence, "If nothing changes, nothing changes." The first things that need to change are your awareness and attitudes about money. In order to conquer your money issues:

1. Admit that you have a problem with spending.

2. Cut self-criticism out immediately. Forgive yourself.

3. Remember that lots of other people deal with this issue, too.

4. Take full responsibility for your financial situation.

5. Resolve to make changes. And mean it.

6. Decide what you want to accomplish, and when.

7. Allow yourself to make some mistakes along the way. No one is perfect. (Even you!)

8. Find nonmonetary ways to treat yourself.

9. Take specific actions, starting with an honest appraisal of your financial position.

Here's where raw honesty and the desire to resolve your money problems give you a jump start. The first step is simple. It may not be easy for you to take the time and make yourself commit this to paper, but it is essential for you to begin right here, at the beginning. You will be taking a complete inventory of your debt and monthly payments. Remember, it really is very simple. And when you're finished, you'll be amazed at how painless it actually was. So pick up your pen and read on.

Take Inventory of Your Debt and Monthly Payments

Here we go! Use the following worksheet as a guide to your complete inventory of debt and monthly payments. It may help to look through your check register or old receipts for dates and amounts. Spend some time with this, and you'll have a solid foundation for building a more manageable financial future. If you skip over this, you may miss out on the most beneficial information you need to begin to empower yourself.

Obligations	Debtor	Interest Rate %	Total Amount	Monthly Payment
Rent or Mortgages				
Home Equity Loans				
Automobile Loans				
Furniture Loans				
Bank Loans				
Installment Loans				
Student Loan #1				
Student Loan #2				
Credit Card #1				
Credit Card #2				
Credit Card #3				
Credit Card #4				
Credit Card #5				
Credit Card #6				
Loans from Family				
Loans from Friends				
Other Debts				
Other Debts				
Other Debts				
Totals				

Even though your rent may not technically be a debt, it is a fixed monthly obligation and is included in calculating your debt. How much debt is too much? The next section shows you how to measure healthy debt.

How to Measure Healthy Debt

The amount of debt that you may handle reasonably well depends on your monthly income. The most significant indicator of unhealthy debt is your percentage of debt payments to your monthly income. Specifically, your percentage of debt payments is calculated as follows:

Total Monthly Debt Payments (from above) ÷ Total Monthly Income = Percentage of Debt Payments

$$\$\underline{\hspace{4cm}} \div \$\underline{\hspace{4cm}} = \underline{\hspace{1cm}} \%$$

After you've calculated your percentage of debt payments, measure your debt health:

HEALTHY	UNHEALTHY	UNMANAGEABLE
0%	25%	35%

If your debt falls in the healthy range, but you still feel burdened or anxious about it, then it is not healthy for you. Is your debt unhealthy or unmanageable? The good news is that even drastically unhealthy or unmanageable debt has a solution. It may take time, attention, and patience, but when you have a plan and work your plan, you will reap the rewards and lift the burden of your debt.

Financial aid counselors advise students to make an appointment anytime they have financial difficulties: "We can always reevaluate their situation. At the very least, we can help them brainstorm solutions. At best, they may be eligible for aid they weren't aware of."

Steps You Can Take Today to Deal with Unhealthy Debt

The single most important thing you can do to deal with unhealthy debt is to eliminate it. Obvious answer, right? Well, not really. Eliminating your debt is never a simple thing to do. And it's usually not something you can choose to do today. Most of us just don't have a stash of cash lying around waiting to pay down debt. However, if you do happen to have the cash, consider these options:

- Pay off the smallest balance first. By doing so, you will most efficiently eliminate one monthly payment.

- Pay off as many small accounts as you can. The more accounts you can eliminate, the more free cash you'll have next month to pay down the rest of your outstanding debt.

- Pay off the accounts with the highest interest rates. This will save you money in the long run by lowering your total interest payments. For example, if you had to choose between paying off a $1,500 credit card debt at 19.8 percent interest or a $1,500 student loan at 7 percent interest, you would save $192 annually by paying off the credit card.

- Pay down loans that accrue interest at a higher rate than the rate you are earning in an investment. In other words, if your credit card accrues interest at 19.8 percent and your investment earns only 6.5 percent, you're better off using that investment money to pay off your debt. If you don't, you are essentially "losing" 13.3 percent every year. On a debt of $2,500, it's costing you $332.50 each year to keep the investment and carry the debt.

- Pay an extra amount on the principal balance every month. Be sure to indicate "principal payment" on the check and remittance advice. (If you don't clearly designate this as a principal payment, it will automatically be applied as a prepayment of your next bill, which is primarily interest.) Never be content to make only the minimum payment.

- Scrape together all the extra cash you can. That's right. You probably have cash in hidden places. It may not look like cash right now, but you can turn it into cash. This is where the determination and discipline come in to the picture. When you resolve to choose debt payment over spending cash, you'll begin to wage real war. It happens when you're focused and creative. Here are some ideas to get you started:

- Go through your closets, storage, car, basement and attic. Advertise a yard sale next Saturday from 8 to 11 A.M. Don't worry about pricing the stuff; just place it about on the lawn. This is usually always good for a quick $100 or more.

- Get rid of that exercise equipment you never use. Place an ad in the classifieds.

- Barter something you would otherwise pay cash for.

  Examples: Work a few hours a week at the health club in exchange for unlimited use. Answer phones at the hair salon in trade for haircut/color/products. It takes only two minutes to ask the owner, and the worst-case reaction is a painless, "No." Even if it doesn't work for that owner, chances are excellent that it will work for their competitor. Try small businesses first.

- Help someone move. Tutor students. House-sit for vacationing neighbors. Shop for the elderly or disabled. Carpool for working moms. Offer your services for baby-sitting, lawn mowing, leaf raking, ironing, cleaning, car washing and detailing (three hours may net you $75 or more). Use your imagination. What are you good at, and what can you do for extra cash right away with no cash investment?

And, of course, you must curtail your spending. I repeat: You must curtail your spending. Take a few minutes and jot down some ideas. What are you spending now that you could do without? Hints: Pizza, cable, videos, clothes, restaurant meals, dry cleaning, manicures, gifts, snacks, and "other stuff." What is your "other stuff"? If you have a difficult time coming up with a list, ask your best friend to help you brainstorm. It's great to have a friend's support, especially when you're making choices about what to do on the weekend, for example.

Use the following chart to take an inventory of the random nonessential things you spend money on in the course of a month. Dare to total up how much of your income you're donating to the local espresso bar. How much do you spend on taxis in the course of a month? And so on. Next to each item, estimate how much you think you spend now and how much you can cut that down to.

Expenditure:	Current Monthly Spending:	Can Cut Amount To:
_____	$_____	$_____
_____	_____	_____
_____	_____	_____
_____	_____	_____
_____	_____	_____
_____	_____	_____
_____	_____	_____
_____	_____	_____
_____	_____	_____
_____	_____	_____
_____	_____	_____
_____	_____	_____
TOTALS:	$_____ (A)	$_____ (B)

To calculate your estimated monthly savings, subtract (B) from (A):

(A) $_____ – (B) $_____ = $_____ savings

Congratulations! You've found cash. Is it enough to stem the increase in your debts and provide cash to pay down the principal balances? If not, keep digging. Your determination and a concerted effort will yield profits. Guaranteed.

CHAPTER 9

You *Can* Cope With Burdensome Debt

You go to a doctor when you have ailments that won't go away. And the more it hurts, the quicker you go. Of course, you don't like going to the doctor. It takes time. It can be expensive. It's just not fun. But when it hurts enough, you go.

If your foot is broken, you go to an orthopedic specialist, not a heart surgeon. The sooner you go to the right person, the sooner you'll get the appropriate treatment to solve your problem. The same is true of solving a financial problem. When you need help with overspending, debt, or credit repair, it's important to clarify the problem and find the resources that specialize in that arena. Ask yourself:

- Have I clearly identified my problem(s)?
- What do I want to achieve, specifically?
- What are the solutions to my problems?
- What services will help me achieve these solutions?

Begin by taking your own inventory of possible solutions and services. You may find that compulsive spending is causing you to go in the financial hole each month. It may be as simple as needing to find a part time job to pay off some debts. Or you may need professional assistance in considering options such as declaring bankruptcy.

Jesse, 27, reports that his problems were so complex that he had to turn to professionals for advice: "But it turned out that my problems weren't as complicated as I thought. I was just overwhelmed by them. The counselor helped me sort them out and put a plan together."

Take a minute now to consider the list below, and add your own solutions:

- You have too many monthly payments.

- Many of your payments are too high.

- Your payments are due sporadically (i.e., quarterly), and might be easier to handle if smaller amounts were billed monthly.

- You love to buy things. You get carried away and can't help it.

- You have a tough time controlling your credit card use.

- You are harassed by bill collectors or lawyers.

- You don't understand why you've been turned down for credit.

- You've never learned how to budget.

- You have a budget, but can't seem to stick to it.

- You resent having a budget. You spend because you feel like it.

- You want to save, but just can't do it.

These problems may feel overwhelming and insurmountable. They're not. Millions of people all over the world face these issues. The difference between those who overcome them and those who don't is simply a matter of taking the appropriate steps now. Whatever challenges you face, help is available to you today, for either a nominal fee or no charge at all.

CREDIT COUNSELORS OFFER VALUABLE SERVICES

Many different resources and services exist in your community to help you navigate these waterways. And just like everything else, some are better than others in terms of their skills and service. So take a bit of time up front to do your homework and ask questions before committing to their plan for you. Here are some questions to answer for each service before you decide whom to use:

- Does this organization specialize in the services I need?

- Have I spoken to several people who have used their services? Were they satisfied? Why or why not?

- Is this a "for-profit" or nonprofit organization? (Nonprofit organizations may be more likely to be consumer advocates.)

- How does this organization make money? Who pays for their services? (This tells you whose interests they will be protecting; yours or your creditors'.)

- How does this organization view bankruptcy as an alternative? (Bankruptcy has serious ramifications for you and your financial future. Use it only as a last resort.)

- How will this organization be involved? Do they only give advice or do they handle it for me?

- How will their actions affect my credit record?

- How long will it stay on my credit record? (It may follow you for seven years or longer.)

- What is the downside of having this on my credit record? Will I be denied credit as a result?

- What alternative choices do I have?

You *do* have alternative choices. That's the good news. It is definitely worth your while to thoroughly explore your options and alternatives. Your are about to make choices that will affect you and your financial life for many years to come. Now is the time to weigh them carefully.

Sorting through the maze to find the right services for you may be the toughest part. To make it as painless as possible, several resources are listed below, along with their address, telephone number, and a brief description of the type of service they offer. Call each one and ask the questions above to find out more. Give them a brief introduction to your problem and the outcomes you want to achieve, then ask if they might be able to help and how.

North American Consumer Alliance (NACA)
6911 South 1300 East, Suite 500
Midvale, UT 84047
(800) 497-NACA
(Nonprofit consumer advocacy group that offers legal services to members with debt, credit, and tax problems.)

Debtors Anonymous
Grand Central Station
P.O. Box 400
New York, NY 10163-0400
(212) 642-8220
(212) 969-8111

Debtors Anonymous—Los Angeles
City National Building, 4th Floor
11500 Olympic Blvd.
Los Angeles, CA 90024
(310) 479-1098
(Support groups and meetings for anyone with compulsive debt or spending problems. Twelve-step orientation. Inquiries are strictly confidential.)

Credi-Care, Inc.
216 Lorna Square
Hoover, AL 35216
(205) 823-8515
(Debt counseling services)

National Foundation for Consumer Credit, Inc. (a.k.a. Consumer Credit Counselors)
8701 Georgia Ave.
Silver Springs, MD 20910
(301) 589-5600
(800) 388-2227 (Follow the recorded instructions)
(Nonprofit organization that offers help with debt reorganization and creditor negotiation.)

Budget and Credit Counseling Services
55 Fifth Avenue, 13th Floor
New York, NY 10003

(212) 675-5070
(Debt counseling service)
Legal Services Corporation of America
(Free legal advice to those with financial need. Most states and counties have participating legal aid offices. Look in the phone directory under Legal Services or Attorneys. States and counties may have different names for their free legal aid offices. Or look up your Chamber of Commerce or county court house for assistance.)

Cooperative Extension
(If you live in a rural area, consider contacting this educational network, which combines the resources of the federal government, universities, and 3,100 county offices. Call your county offices or a land-grant University near you for details.)

Consumer Affairs or Consumer Protection Bureaus
(Offered by most city or county governments, services vary, primarily to protect consumer rights. Look in the blue pages of your phone book for locations and telephone numbers.)

IS BANKRUPTCY A GOOD OPTION?

Filing for bankruptcy is a last-ditch resort, to be contemplated only after you've tried everything else . . . at least once. No ifs, ands, or buts about it. Period.

Now, if you still want to know more, here it is. Bankruptcy is generally a three-step process:

1. When you have no assets to pay your debts (and no hope for other solutions), you file a petition in federal or state court declaring that you're insolvent.

2. You work with the court to devise a repayment plan.

3. Your creditors generally receive some money, though usually not the full amount.

Individuals may file for bankruptcy in two standard ways:

Chapter 7 bankruptcy: You seek to be released of all your debts after selling all your assets to pay creditors. The home you own is exempt from sale. Some debts, however, such as student loans, taxes, alimony, and fines must still be paid. Chapter 7 bankruptcy is allowed only once in a six-year period. Use of an attorney is advisable, though not required.

Chapter 13 bankruptcy: You may retain your property and pay your creditors over a three to five year period using your wages. Partial payment is often arranged to satisfy the debt in full. Some income, such as child support, is excluded. The court must approve and supervise the plan. Use of an attorney is required.

Bankruptcy Pros

1. You can avoid losing your home.
2. It protects you against the IRS seizing your property for back taxes.
3. It provides legal protection from your creditors.
4. It provides you with the chance to start again.

Bankruptcy Cons

1. It seriously harms your credit rating—for a long, long time.
2. Some debts will remain outstanding and you must pay them.
3. You lose privacy; bankruptcies are often published in the newspaper.
4. You involve the judicial system, thereby losing control and increasing costs.
5. You lose assets, at the direction of the court and not of your own choosing.

Although the idea of being discharged from at least part of your debts may seem extremely appealing to you, bankruptcy can actually increase your financial difficulties. Thousands of people regret filing bankruptcy because they under estimated the severe long-term financial impact on their financial life. Many lost most or all of their assets, and they often didn't get the full relief from debt that they anticipated. In short, it wasn't all it was cracked up to be. While poor credit ratings can stay on your credit report for seven years, bankruptcies can stay with you for ten years after they're discharged. Bankruptcy is a financial burden far greater than slow payment.

However, there is one positive footnote worth mentioning, according to the financial aid director at a large university: "A previous bankruptcy does not necessarily preclude your chances of obtaining a student loan in the future." So take heart, and know that the world is not coming to an end if you do have a bankruptcy.

LOAN CONSOLIDATION: IS IT THE RIGHT ANSWER?

Loan consolidation appears to be a very simple solution. Just roll all your debts into one, with lower monthly payments and a longer payout. You'll owe only one company and avoid the barrage of bills, collectors, and harassment. It's tempting, indeed. But does it really work, and is it the right solution for you?

Consider the flip side. The interest rates may be very high. If your current debts have relatively low interest rates, with loan consolidation you could conceivably pay more interest in the long run, thereby making it much more expensive overall. To top that off, they often impose stiff prepayment penalties, so that if you pay the balance off early, you're zapped with additional charges that make it even more costly. It's clearly an expensive trade-off that allows you to ease your financial pressures only in the short term. You wind up paying more later. Consider it only as a drastic measure to avoid filing bankruptcy.

If you find that loan consolidation is an attractive option even after considering the pitfalls, then you will want to put together a game plan and investigate several sources. Start by formulating your request and a plausible payment plan. Include these points and be ready to give out copies of this information and answer a lot of questions:

- Make a comprehensive list of all your cash income sources and amounts.

- Make a comprehensive lists of all your debts (see the section called "Take Inventory of Your Debt and Monthly Payments" in chapter 8), including;
  Creditor name, address, phone number, and contact name
  Account number
  Interest rate
  Balance due
  Amount currently past due
  Current payment schedule
  Number of payments until final payoff
  Date of projected final payment under current payment schedule
  Total of all monthly payments
  Total of all outstanding debts

- Support this list with copies of each creditor's bill or statement.

- Propose an alternative reduced monthly payment amount that is reasonable and affordable, given your monthly cash income.

- List possible collateral items. They should not be attached to any loans or other debts. Ideas include:
  Your car
  Your savings or investments (Consider using these to pay down the debt.)
  Jewelry
  Your home
  Anything with market value that you own outright and prefer not to sell

Your ability to find a consolidation loan will also depend on your credit history, stability in your rental and/or job history, the amount of money you are requesting, your income sources, and loan counselors' perceptions of your integrity. You will help yourself enormously by gathering evidence of any of these things in advance and including them in your request. Thorough planning and preparation will impress them with your determination and give them additional confidence that you will follow through and repay the loan.

Now that you've put your request together, you're ready to approach any number of potential loan sources. Start with the ones that seem most likely, and be prepared to hear, "No, I'm sorry." Rejection may be hard to take, but it's important to ask them for a clear reason in a nondefensive tone. Perhaps you may be able to overcome their objection. If not, you will learn something that will be useful in changing your plan, changing your approach, or changing whom you ask. Here are your options:

Family and Friends
Especially if you have no credit history, loans from friends or family may be the easiest way to get the money you need. But beware: handle them just like a banking business transaction, or good relationships can sour fast. Document the transaction in a formal note, detailing all of the terms and expectations. Have each party sign it and keep a copy.

Tips: • Offer them above-market interest rates (more than they receive on investments).

Pros: • It may be easy to appeal to their understanding of your integrity.

• You may be able to get part of the total from two or more individuals.

Cons: • Failure to repay on time could harm your relationship.

Employer Loans

Most employers have strict policies against making loans to employees. If your employer allows the practice, you'll want to protect yourself with a formal document spelling out all the terms and conditions. Remember, if the loan causes ill feelings, you can jeopardize your job. Ask about regular payroll deductions to pay it back over time, giving each of you greater peace of mind.

Tips: • Your chances are best if your company is small and you can ask the owner directly.

• This type of loan may not be feasible if your company is not extremely employee oriented.

Pros: • Interest rates may be much lower than any most other sources.

Cons: • Most employers frown on granting employees loans.

• Failure to pay timely may jeopardize your job.

Banks and Savings & Loans

Consumer loans are an important part of their business, and timely repayment may be an excellent way to establish a good credit record if you have none. Rates will vary dramatically, depending on the amount, type, and length of the loan. They may also require some type of significant collateral.

Tips: • If you or your family has significant business there, they may be more willing to help.

• Small community banks that know you may be better prospects.

Pros: • They may have more programs and options for you to consider.

Cons: • Interest rates tend to be higher than credit unions.

Credit Unions

Loans from credit unions are often less expensive than from traditional lending institutions, but you must be a member to utilize their services.

Tips: • An estimated 60–70 percent of all adults are eligible to become members of credit unions.

• Only half of all eligible adults are currently members of credit unions.

- To find out the names of credit unions that might accept you as a new member, call the Credit Union National Association at (800) 356-9655.

Pros: • Credit unions never charge prepayment penalties.

Cons: • You must have a savings account at the credit union to be eligible.

Finance Companies

These are private companies in business to lend money to consumers. They often prey upon people who have bad credit and charge exorbitant rates. Watch out for shark-infested waters!

Tips: • Try to get your loan elsewhere, first.

Pros: • They're more flexible because they are not encumbered by federal banking regulations.

Cons: • Some type of asset for collateral is usually required.

• Due to the high risk, you generally pay much higher interest rates.

Pawn Shops

This should be your last resort. Pawnshops are legitimate businesses, regulated by law, but their rates are not attractive unless you have exhausted all other options.

Tips: • Beware! They typically lend only 25 percent to 50 percent of an item's value.

Pros: • You may pawn an asset and receive cash very quickly and easily.

Cons: • Interest rates may be as high as 25% per month or 300% per year.

• If you fail to pay the interest and redeem your asset, it will be sold.

Home Equity Loans

Home equity loans are available from traditional financial institutions as well as finance companies. Typically, you may borrow up to 80 percent of the equity in your home. Some offer more than that, with impeccable credit. Home equity loans should not be used for unnecessary expenditures, such as vacations.

Tips: • Interest rates are often variable. Find out what the rate is tied to and when it fluctuates.

Pros: • Interest rates may be lower than credit cards.

• The interest you pay may be tax deductible.

Cons: • Your home may be foreclosed for nonpayment.

HOW TO WORK WITH CREDITORS ON YOUR OWN

Have you been avoiding your creditors, leaving their letters unanswered and their phone calls unreturned? Although it's a natural reaction, this approach has a profoundly destructive effect, serving only to increase their frustration and create anger toward you. Your job is now clear: Open the lines of communication and give them a reason to want to help you. They will be eager to work with you if:

1. You have a plausible explanation for your delinquent payments.

2. They believe you are sincere in your desire to pay them.

3. They believe they may lose out if filing bankruptcy is a potential outcome.

4. You have an alternative payment plan worked out that demonstrates your good intentions and effort.

You can accomplish all this in one simple, standard letter that is personalized and mailed to each creditor on your list. Sort of like asking a professor to extend an assignment, you can ask creditors to extend a new payment plan. By arranging a lower monthly payment with each creditor, you will significantly relieve your monthly cash flow burden and salvage your credit rating. Thousands of people do this every day, with outstanding results. Use the form at the end of the chapter as a guide.

Sample Letter to Creditors
Request for Lower Monthly Payments

Date

Credit Manager's Name
Creditor Company Name
Street Address
City, State, Zip

Dear (Credit Manager's Name),

As of (date), my account (account #) with your company has a balance of ($ amount). Because I recently experienced (large unexpected medical bills, unemployment, or other reason for hardship), my payments have been (slow/erratic/overdue). I am anxious to preserve my good credit and arrange an acceptable alternative payment plan with you, beginning immediately.

I am able to pay ($ amount) each month until the balance is paid off in (# of) months. This amount is manageable for me and my financial plan. The first payment is enclosed. I will increase the amount of my payment as my cash flow allows.

Your cooperation will be tremendously helpful as I work to avoid the alternative of bankruptcy. Thank you for your confidence and patience. Please call me if you need to discuss this further.

Sincerely,

Your name
Street Address
City, State, Zip
(Area Code) Phone Number

CHAPTER 10

Take Charge of Your Credit Report

Whether or not you realize it, your everyday life is affected by your credit report and the historical information it contains about you. Credit information significantly impacts your ability to get an apartment, buy a car, get insurance, and even get a job. In fact, some dating services now *pull credit reports!*

Tracking the credit history of American consumers has become a $150 billion industry, with computerized records of over 150 million individuals. Businesses request and scrutinize more than 400 million credit reports every year—1.1 million each day!

Your credit history is kept by credit bureaus as a record of how well you paid your debts in the past and serves as a predictor of how well you will pay in the future. Credit reports routinely contain errors. You are ultimately responsible for the accuracy of your credit report, as one person we surveyed reports.

"Collection agencies and credit departments kept calling me to collect debts I didn't owe. It turns out that they confused me with someone else who has the same name. They even sent late pay reports to my credit report. I found out about it when I applied for a card and got turned down. It took months to correct my credit report." —Jesse, 24

It's important to realize that information on your credit report usually stays there for seven years or longer. Think of it as your financial report card. It contains information such as:

- Your name
- Your birth date
- Your address

- Your social security number
- Your spouse's name
- Your employer
- Your credit payment history on:
  - All major credit cards (Visa, MasterCard, Discover, etcetera)
  - American Express and Diners Club cards
  - Major national retail accounts (Sears, J. C. Penney, etcetera)
  - Finance company loans
  - Auto loans
  - Bank loans
  - Student loans paid to a bank
- Inquiries by creditors
- Collection agency efforts
- Bankruptcies
- Foreclosures
- Financial judgements
- Tax liens
- Child support payments, if late

Unless a collection agency has been involved, your credit report does not usually contain:

- Your salary
- Utility accounts
- Medical bills
- Landlord collections
- Attorney bills

Credit bureaus are at the center of the credit reporting system. They collect and organize credit information, distributing it to the businesses that subscribe to their service, as well as consumers who request it. Along with 1,200 local and regional credit bureaus, three major national bureaus control most of the credit information disseminated to creditors.

When evaluating your credit-worthiness, creditors analyze your credit report and apply their own scoring system to the information it contains. From this score, they come up with an estimate of how big a credit risk you are. Unfortunately, errors in credit information abound, and they often create huge headaches for consumers.

In the late '80s and early '90s, several independent studies revealed that between 42 and 50 percent of all credit reports contain errors. Credit bureaus process an astounding 2 billion transactions every month. With that kind of volume, it's no wonder that errors occur. But it's largely up to you to find and correct the errors. That's why it's important for you to know exactly what the credit bureaus are reporting about you, and make sure it's accurate.

HOW TO GET YOUR CREDIT REPORT

There's nothing mysterious or complicated about obtaining copies of your credit reports from the three major bureaus. After calling them to confirm the address and fee, simply send a letter (suggested format below) with the appropriate fee and information.

TRW
P.O. Box 749-029
Dallas, TX 75374
(800) 392-1122
(First report free)

Equifax Information Service
P.O. Box 740193
Atlanta, GA 30374-0193
(800) 685-1111
($8 per report + local sales tax)

Trans Union
P.O. Box 80700
North Olmsted, OH 44070-8070
(800) 922-5490
($8 per report + local sales tax)

Credit Report Letter

Date

Credit Bureau Name
Street Address
City, State, Zip

To Customer Service;

Enclosed is my ($ amount) money order for a complete copy of my credit report. Please send it to:
    (Your full legal name)
    (Your address)

I am enclosing a copy of my (driver's license/social security card/state ID card/etcetera) as proof of identification.

Sincerely,

(Your signature here)

(Your full legal name)
(Your current address)
(Your phone number)
(Your social security number)
(Your birth date)

Tips and pointers for sending your letters effectively:

1. Keep copies of all letters.

2. Mail them certified return receipt (for proof that you sent them and they received them).

3. Pay by money order to expedite processing.

4. Allow four weeks to receive your report.

5. If you don't receive them in four weeks, copy the original letter, write "Second Request" boldly in red, and send again.

If you'd prefer to write only one letter, you may send $30.95 along with a completed application to Credco Inc., and receive a merged file of all three credit reports. For a copy of the application, call Credco Inc. at (800) 637-2422. For your convenience in disputing an item on your credit report, they'll also send you a dispute form.

WHAT YOUR CREDIT REPORT MEANS

The three major credit bureaus all report their information in slightly different formats. Technically, they may appear in different styles, but they essentially all convey the same information. Basically, each one tells the story about:

- The type and number of your creditors
- The current status of outstanding balances on your accounts
- Lateness patterns in your past payments

Specifically, you will find some common information in all three formats:

- Name of creditor
- Creditor's address
- Account number
- Date account opened
- Joint or individual account
- Payment type
- Credit limit

- Current balance owing
- Amount past due, if any
- Payment history
- Date of last update

As you might guess, creditors interpret this information by drawing conclusions about patterns they see. They're looking for evidence of stability, consistency, and dependability. In short, creditors want to know: Do you have a reliable history? Are you likely to pay your bills on time every time? Do you have enough credit to prove this, but not too much to cause potentially overwhelming debt?

Red Flags
No scoring system in the world can possibly predict this with complete accuracy, but creditors generally agree that these factors serve as warning flags. Their presence usually decreases your overall score and reduces your chances of obtaining additional credit at favorable terms:

- Too many accounts
- Too few accounts
- High outstanding balances
- Slow payments
- Credit counseling history
- Debt collection efforts
- Charge-offs (debts discharged through bankruptcy)
- Bankruptcy
- Low income
- New business employer
- Frequent employer changes
- Business address same as home address
- P.O. Box address
- Frequent address changes

Green Lights
Indicators of reliability include the opposites of the above items, along with:

- Checking and/or savings accounts
- IRA and/or investment accounts
- Auto ownership

KNOW YOUR RIGHTS

As a consumer, your credit rights are protected under several federal and state laws. They include the Fair Credit Reporting Act, the Equal Credit Opportunity Act, the Truth in Lending Act, and the Fair Credit Billing Act. By familiarizing yourself with them, you will empower yourself with the tools you need to combat errors and enhance your credit rating.

Fair Credit Reporting Act

The Fair Credit Reporting Act gives you tools for credit repair. Under this act, you have the right to:

1. Obtain a copy of your credit report.

2. Receive the report free of charge within 30 days of being denied credit.

3. Receive the report for a reasonable fee, if no credit denial.

4. Find out who has received copies of your report in the past.

5. Have erroneous information investigated and corrected, if appropriate.

6. Request that additional information be inserted in your file.

7. Have your version of a dispute be included in the record and distributed along with the report.

8. Sue for damages when a company willfully violates the law, and to collect attorney's fees and court costs.

Equal Credit Opportunity Act

This law establishes fairness for consideration of credit applications. Under the Equal Credit Opportunity Act you have the right to:

1. Find out why you were denied credit.

2. Establish credit in your own name.

3. Not be denied credit on the basis of your:
   • age
   • sex
   • marital status

- race
- color
- religion
- national origin

4. Have sources such as alimony and child support considered as any other income.

Truth in Lending Act

The Truth in Lending Act spells out consumers' rights to loan information. It gives you the right to:

1. Receive a complete, written explanation of the annual percentage rate (APR) and the total dollar amount of the transaction.

2. Rescind contracts within 3 days in certain circumstances.

Fair Credit Billing Act

Fair Credit Billing Act established the procedures required of creditors to correct mistakes. It gives you the right to:

1. Withhold payment of any disputed portion of a bill until it is resolved.

2. Receive acknowledgment from the creditor within 30 days.

3. Resolve the dispute within two billing cycles.

How to Repair Your Credit Report

Under the Fair Credit Reporting Act, you have the right to dispute any entry on your credit report that you "reasonably believe" to be erroneous or incomplete. Creditors must respond to your challenge within a reasonable period of time, but are not forced to make changes. The Federal Trade Commission interprets a reasonable period of time as 30 days. If an investigation of the facts results in a finding of error, the credit bureau must correct your credit report or delete the information. This is the process that Jesse, the person with the mistaken identity problem mentioned earlier in the chapter, went through to correct his credit report.

The secret to successfully disputing credit report information is in the wording of the dispute letter. Never make excuses or give reasons for late payments. Your objective is to point out errors, inaccuracies, and/or incomplete reports. Tailor the sample dispute claims below to your specific situation, or apply the style and tone to draft your own verbiage.

"I do not have two accounts with this creditor. One of the entries appears to be a duplicate. Please correct this error."

"The balance on this account is not past due. Please investigate and correct the error."

"I am not married. Please correct this inaccuracy."

"The report erroneously lists my social security number as XXX-XX-XXXX. My correct social security number is XXX-XX-XXXX."

"I did not authorize this company to inquire into my credit history. Please remove this inquiry."

"I have always paid this account as agreed. Please investigate your erroneous record of late payment and correct or delete this information."

"This account is not mine. Please delete it."

The Fair Credit Reporting Act gives you the right to add to your credit report a descriptive statement of 100 words or fewer explaining the extenuating circumstances of any item in your report. Were your credit cards stolen and used? Are you disputing a billing error? Was the quality of the service or merchandise you received unacceptable? Did unexpected circumstances put you in a financial bind? This is your opportunity to officially explain significant items to your creditors and potential creditors.

If the credit bureau does not have a standard dispute form, it may help to use the letter format at the end of the chapter, inserting your own details and descriptive information:

You may wait up to six weeks to hear from the credit bureau on the results of their investigation. If you don't hear from them, repeat the cycle. Be sure to keep copies of all your correspondence and send each one via certified, return-receipt mail.

Credit Bureau Dispute Letter

Date

Credit Bureau Name
Street Address
City, State, Zip

To Customer Service:

I received a copy of my credit report dated (date). On that date, the following items were erroneous or incomplete:

1. Regarding (account name, number, outstanding amount), (insert description and action requested to correct).
2. Regarding . . . etcetera

Additionally, in accordance with my rights under the Fair Credit Reporting Act, I request that you insert the following consumer statements into my credit report:

   (Your statement of 100 words or less)

Please update my report accordingly and send a copy of my corrected report to:

(Your name and address or those of any creditors you wish to update)

Thank you for your prompt attention.

Sincerely,

(Your name)
(Street address)
(City, State, Zip)
(Social security number)

CHAPTER *11*

Dealing With Collection Agencies

Collection agencies are often very intimidating and powerful sounding. Most people are surprised to find out that in reality, collection agencies have little or no power. They are just companies in the business of collecting money for others. They're paid by their clients (the company that gave credit) based on what they collect. Their cut is usually at least half. That's why they use fear and intimidation tactics. And often, they use scary threats that sound official. But they have no official power themselves. All they can do is report you to someone else—usually the credit bureau.

FIND OUT WHO YOU'RE DEALING WITH AND WHAT THEY'RE REPORTING

Collection agencies constantly call and harass you at all hours. They stoop to interrogating others when you're not home. It's so disturbing that you've begun to screen your calls. Or worse, you get so many threatening phone calls from bill collectors that you cringe every time the phone rings. But you don't have to put up with everything they might dish out.

> "Collection agencies are so rude and inconsiderate. They'll do anything to get at you. One time they harassed my roommate and had her in tears. She had nothing to do with my problem. I was furious!"—Julia, 21

Although we may not be aware of it, a very powerful and underutilized law fully protects consumers from undue harassment and abuse. On September 20, 1977, The Fair Debt Collection Practices Act (FDCPA) was passed into Public Law 95-108. It was subsequently updated and amended on July 9, 1986 by Public Law 99-361. Collection agencies are required by the FDCPA to:

- Clearly identify themselves, including the name of their company and their own name.

- Explain specifically why they are calling, giving you:
  The creditor's name
  The account number
  The exact amount you owe

- Mail you a letter within five days of their first contact, detailing:
  The name of the creditor you owe
  The exact amount you owe
  Steps for you to take if you wish to dispute the debt

If you receive collection calls and they don't follow these standards, they are violating the FDCPA. You have every right to ask them for complete disclosure of this information.

KNOW YOUR RIGHTS

Do you know your rights under federal credit and collection laws? If not, you're in the 90 percent majority of Americans who don't. Together, the important pieces of legislation under the FDCPA protect your rights and give you the leverage you need to defend yourself against undue force from bill collectors.

Collection Agency No-Nos

In summary, collection agencies are strictly prohibited from:

- Using the telephone repeatedly to annoy any person

- Calling before 8:00 A.M. or after 9:00 P.M. without your permission

- Calling you at work if they are aware that your employer disapproves

- Forcing you to accept collect calls or pay for telegrams

- Contacting you by post card

- Using a false name or identity

- Using profane or obscene language

- Harassing and /or verbally abusing you or any others

- Threatening you with violence

- Threatening any harm to any person or their reputation or property

- Threatening any actions that may not be legally carried out

- Falsely implying that they are an attorney or representative of the government

- Sending any correspondence that resembles an official court or government document

- Falsely implying that they work for a credit bureau

- Falsely implying that you have committed a crime

- Implying that you will be arrested if you do not pay your bill

- Threatening to seize, garnish, attach, or sell your property or wages unless they intend to follow through and it is legal for them to do so

- Contacting any third parties (except your lawyer, credit bureaus, and people who might help locate you)

- Telling a third party that you owe money

- Misrepresenting the amount of your debt

- Mailing you anything that indicates on the outside of the envelope that it is a debt collection effort

- Publishing lists of consumers who do not pay

- Giving out false credit information about you

- Collecting amounts greater than your debt, unless allowed by law

- Depositing a postdated check early

If you feel that bill collectors have transgressed the standards of the FDCPA and your rights have been violated, you can get help. Although they are not allowed to intervene in individual disputes, the Federal Trade Commission (FTC) can help answer your questions about your rights under the FDCPA. Contact any of these FTC offices:

Federal Trade Commission—National Offices
6th St. and Pennsylvania Ave. NW
Washington, D.C. 20580
(202) 326-3224

FTC—Regional Office (AL, FL, GA, MS, NC, SC, TN, VA)
60 Forth St. SW, Suite 5M-35
Atlanta, GA 30303-2322
(404) 656-1399

FTC—Regional Office (CT, ME, MA, NH, RI, VT)
101 Merrimac St.
Boston, MA 02114
(617) 424-5960

FTC—Regional Office (IL, IN, IA, KY, MN, MO, WI)
55 E. Monroe St., Suite 1860
Chicago, IL 60603
(312) 353-8156

FTC—Regional Office (DE, MD, MI, OH, PA, WV)
1111 Superior Ave., Suite 200
118 St. Clair Avenue
Cleveland, OH 44114
(216) 263-3455

FTC—Regional Office (AR, LA, NM, OK, TX)
1999 Bryan St., Suite 2150
Dallas, TX 75201
(214) 979-0213

FTC—Regional Office (CO, KS, MT, NE, ND, SD, UT, WY)
1961 Stout St., Suite 1523
Denver, CO 80294
(303) 844-2272

FTC—Regional Office (AZ, So. CA)
11000 Wilshire Blvd.
Los Angeles, CA 90024
(310) 235-4040

FTC—Regional Office (NJ, NY)
150 William St., 13th Fl.
New York, NY 10038
(212) 264-1207

FTC—Regional Office (No. CA, HA, NV)
901 Market St., Suite 570
San Francisco, CA 94103
(415) 356-5270

FTC—Regional Office (AL, ID, OR, WA)
915 Second Avenue, Suite 2896
Seattle, WA 98174
(206) 220-6350

YOU CAN STOP THE HARASSMENT

Once you have established that a collector has violated your rights under the FDCPA, your first step is to document the violations in as much detail as possible. Make a list that includes specific dates, times, names, actions, words, and phrases, and witnesses, if any. Keep this list for your own possible use in the future. Then draft a letter to the head of the collection agency, demanding that these actions cease. It is not necessary to cite any specific violations from your list.

> "My credit counselor showed me how to stop the calls and harassment. Good thing I did it, because my roommate was about ready to move out. I can't pay for this place alone."—Julia, 21

Under the FDCPA, all collection agencies are prohibited from making any further contact with you after they receive your cease-and-desist letter. Use the sample letter at the end of the chapter to draft your own. Consider sending it via certified, return-receipt mail.

After the collection agency receives a cease-and-desist letter, they are prohibited from contacting you for the purpose of collecting the debt. However, they are permitted to notify you that:

1. There will be no further contact regarding the debt.
2. A specific action will be taken, such as turning the account over to an attorney for collection.

It is highly advisable for you to immediately deal with the creditor directly to resolve the debt and avoid attorney involvement on the collection side.

TAKE ACTION TO PROTECT YOURSELF

As indicated in the cease-and-desist letter, you have the option of pursuing legal action against violators of the FDCPA for actual damages, additional damages up to $1,000, reimbursement of court costs, and reimbursement of reasonable attorney's fees. If you decide to pursue your case through the judicial system, the cost of retaining an attorney may far exceed the potential judgment. Try to find an attorney who is willing to take your case in return for the amount awarded in court, if any. Or you may qualify for free legal assistance from a local legal aid program.

Many states have their own laws protecting consumers in matters of debt collection. Contact your state attorney general's office to register your complaint and seek assistance. And it's a good idea to register complaints with your local consumer protection office as well as the local Better Business Bureau. By doing so, you may be helping to protect other consumers from experiencing similar injustices.

By the way, the American Collector's Association (ACA) is the debt collection industry's trade association. Their primary function is to "self-police" the industry and investigate complaints from consumers. You may write to them at:

American Collector's Association (ACA)
P.O. Box 35106
Minneapolis, MN 55435

Letter to Collection Agency

Date

Collection Company President's Name
Name of Collection Company
Street Address
City, State, Zip

Dear (Name),

Under the authority of the Fair Debt Collection Practices Act, I hereby officially demand that you immediately cease and desist all communication with me regarding the following account(s):

(List account names and numbers here)

If you continue to contact me, I will file detailed complaints with the Federal Trade Commission, the state Attorney General, and the Better Business Bureau. Additionally, I will take legal action and assert my rights under the Fair Debt Collection Practices Act to sue for damages, court costs, and attorney's fees.

Do not report erroneous information regarding this debt to any credit bureau or I will take legal action against your violation of my rights under the Fair Credit Reporting Act.

Sincerely,

Your Name
Street Address
City, State, Zip

$ECTION 3
Major Financial Commitments

CHAPTER *12*

Financing Your Education

As you know, college is astoundingly expensive! Four years at the average state university currently costs about $32,000, while four years at the average private university easily exceeds $100,000. The cost of graduate or professional school is equally daunting. These days, a law school student is likely to emerge from law school $66,000 in debt, while medical school students typically incur $75,000 in debt before graduation.

In this chapter, we'll look at the cost of education from two angles:

- Managing your student loans
- Paying for graduate school

STRATEGIES FOR REPAYING STUDENT LOANS

No doubt you have been counseled about the grisly consequences of defaulting on your student loans. Failing to repay your federally subsidized student loans can wreck your credit history, embroil you in a law suit, or disqualify you from federal employment, for starters.

Since federal law requires that students be counseled on the implications of taking student loans, you should already be aware that you are required to repay your loans. But you may not know about some helpful strategies for repaying your student loans. For example, did you know that you can actually reduce the overall cost of your student loan debt by enrolling in special repayment incentive programs offered by many lenders?

Paying on Time Can Save You Money

Depending on who holds your loan and when you received your loan funds, you may be eligible for some or all of these perks:

Lowered interest rate for timely payments: You may be entitled to a reduction in the interest rate on your loans for making a certain number of monthly payments on time.

Loan fee refund: You probably paid a fee to the lender when you borrowed money for school. Some lenders will give you a credit for a portion of the fees you paid for making a certain number of monthly payments on time.

Lowered interest rate for electronic payments: You may be able to get the interest rate on your loans reduced if you arrange to have your monthly payments transferred electronically.

Taking advantage of these programs can save you hundreds, even thousands, of dollars in interest and fees depending on the size of your loans. The details and availability of these programs vary depending on who holds your student loan, so to find out more about programs like those mentioned above, call the agency that sends you the bills for your student loans.

You Can Work Out A Payment Schedule with Your Lender

Paying back your student loans can be tough, but there are programs to make it easier. There are alternatives to the standard ten-year repayment plan for federal loans.

Interest-only payments: If you're experiencing financial problems, you may be able to arrange to pay just the interest on your loans for a certain amount of time. Ask your lender about this option.

Graduated payments: In this program, you can arrange for lower payments at the beginning of the standard ten-year repayment cycle, when your salary is likely to be lower. The payments automatically increase through the years.

Deferments: Under certain conditions, repayment of federally subsidized student loans may be deferred for a maximum of three years. Deferments are authorized for certain activities or situations such as service in the armed forces or Peace Corps, returning to school more than half time, or being unemployed. Generally, the government will pay the interest on the loan during these specific authorized periods.

To apply for a deferment, send a written letter to the lender, detailing your specific circumstances. Keep in mind that you must continue to make payments while you are waiting for an answer to your deferment request.

Forbearance: If you don't qualify for deferment, but still can't make the monthly payments, you may ask the lender for forbearance. If the lender agrees, you can work out an arrangement whereby you stop making payments temporararily, get extra time to make payments, or make smaller scheduled payments. Interest on the loan continues to accrue at the regular rate during the forbearance period, though. Contact the lender directly with a detailed letter.

Loan consolidation: If your student loan debt is substantial, you may be able to combine several federal loans into one larger loan with a longer repayment schedule. Besides giving you more time to pay back your loans, loan consolidation makes payment more convenient if you're merging loans from more than one source. If you're interested, find out if your student loan provider— the agency that is servicing your loan—participates in the federal loan consolidation program. If your lender doesn't participate, you can shop around and arrange a consolidation loan through a lender that does.

When You Can't Make the Payments

If you can't handle the monthly payment schedule established by your lender, find out which programs they can offer to reduce your payments for the short run. As you have seen, there are variety of programs out there to help people make their required payments on time. But remember, by enrolling in such programs, you may increase the amount of interest you will pay over the long run.

If you're having problems repaying your student loan, communicate with your lender. It's in your lender's best interest to work with you to find a way to repay the loan. For more tips on debt management, see chapter 9, "You *Can* Cope With Burdensome Debt."

STRATEGIES FOR PAYING FOR GRADUATE SCHOOL

Here are some tips for financing graduate or professional school.

Pay Off Your Debts Before Applying for Financial Aid

When you apply for financial aid, student assets are assessed at 35 percent. So if you have money stashed away in a savings account, for example, you'll be expected to contribute 35 percent of your savings towards the cost of your education. This figure is the same even if you have student loans. Any debts that you owe (student loans, credit card debts, car loans, etcetera) are not considered when calculating your financial aid eligibility.

Consider the following example:

	Student A	Student B
Savings	$10,000	$1,000
– Debt	$15,000	$0
Net Worth	– $5,000	$1,000
Student's contribution from assets:	$3,500	$350
	($10,000 x 35%)	(1,000 x 35%)

Student A has a lower net worth than Student B, but is expected to contribute more to school because she has more assets available. Her savings are considered a resource for paying for her education, but her obligations are not taken into account under current financial aid formulas.

Pay Higher Interest Loans First
You should always pay down your debts so that you pay off the highest interest rate debts first.

Pay Unsubsidized Loans First
Some of your student loan debt may be subsidized by the federal government (such as loans made through the subsidized Stafford program and the Perkins loan program). When you return to school, even if you are attending only half time, your subsidized loans will go into a period of "deferment" and will again be subsidized so that you pay no interest while you are in school. For this reason, your priority should be paying off those debts which will continue to accrue interest while you are in school.

FINANCIAL AID BASICS

Paying for school has gotten tougher, but help is still available. If you are pursuing a graduate education or continuing your undergraduate degree, you may be eligible for a number of programs offered by the federal government, your state government, the school you're applying to, and private organizations.

You may be eligible for grants, loans, or work-study. You may also receive aid on the basis of your financial need, your merit, or both. (All federal aid programs are awarded on the basis of need only.)

Grants and Scholarships

For students with financial "need," grants are offered by the federal government, state governments, colleges and universities, alumni organizations, and a wide variety of other organizations. Grants do not have to be repaid, and are considered gifts. Think of them as "free money."

Work-Study

Many jobs on campus are available to students receiving financial aid. In college-sponsored work-study programs, the college financial aid office determines which students are eligible to participate in the program and how much they are eligible to earn. Students apply for work-study jobs as they would for other on-campus jobs. Because the federal government funds 70 percent of salaries paid through work-study, these jobs are more plentiful on campus. Nonetheless, it's up to the student to find a job after he or she gets a work-study award.

Loans

The school's financial aid office determines a student's eligibility for guaranteed student loans based on criteria established by the federal government. Most loans have a lower-than-market rate of interest and are to be repaid by the student after graduation.

Loans play an increasingly larger role in financing education. More specifically, federal loan programs, such as the Stafford program, have been instrumental in making education, especially graduate education, accessible to students. Graduate students are eligible for up to $18,500 per year in a Stafford loan as long as their cost of attending school for one year is $18,500 or higher. Plus, depending on the student's "demonstrated need," up to $8,500 of that amount can be subsidized by the federal government, meaning that the government will pay the interest on the loan while the student is in school and for six months after graduation.

Undergraduate students are eligible for smaller amounts of the Stafford loan, depending on their year in school and dependency status. Also, the parents of undergraduates ar eligible to apply for federal loans through the PLUS program.

For more information on all these loans, or for help with the application process, you can call Kaplan's student loan information program at 1-888-KAP-LOAN.

Finding "Free Money"

Grants and scholarships are the best kind of aid to receive, of course, but "free money" can be hard to find on a graduate level. Here are some tips for increasing your odds.

Do a scholarship search. You don't need to pay a scholarship search organization to find potential scholarship resources. Check out free searches on the Internet. A good place to start is www.finaid.org. Visit or call your college financial aid office and the financial aid offices of your prospective schools. Spend some time in the library checking out scholarship books.

Apply to your school as early as possible. Speak to reps of the schools you are interested in to get an idea of how much institutional aid they usually award for the program you hope to attend and what your chances are of receiving some of those funds.

APPLYING FOR FINANCIAL AID

The financial aid application process can be very time consuming, and often confusing for students. If you plan to continue your education and will need help finding money for school, keep the following three things in mind:

- Request financial aid applications at the time you request admissions applications. Do not wait until you get an acceptance letter to apply for aid unless you school specifically tells you to.

- Obtain and file the FAFSA (Free Application for Federal Student Aid) You can get a FAFSA from any college financial aid office or by calling (800) 4-FED-AID.

- Meet all filing deadlines set by your school.

Applying for Aid: Ten Steps

1. Request financial aid applications and instructions at the same time as you request your admissions applications.

2. Make a list of the names and deadlines of all the documents you're required to submit for financial aid evaluation.

FAFSA (Free Application for Federal Student Aid)—required by all schools to evaluate federal aid eligibility, the FAFSA collects basic information regarding income, assets, family size, etcetera. You can get a FAFSA from any college financial aid office or by calling (800) 4-FED-AID.

The College Scholarship Service PROFILE—required by many private schools and scholarship programs, the PROFILE collects more detailed financial information than the FAFSA. You can get a PROFILE registration form from college financial aid offices or by calling (800) 778-6888.

Institutional Aid Applications—required by many schools to determine eligibility for funds from particular schools. You can get these forms from the financial aid offices of the schools you're interested, or, increasingly, find them on the Web.

3. Begin to research scholarship possibilities. Check out free searches on the Internet. Be wary of paying a scholarship search organization for information that is available free elsewhere, especially if they're charging more than 25–40 dollars.

4. Collect financial records such as your most recent tax returns, W-2 forms, records of untaxed income, bank and investment statements, home mortgage statements, business tax forms, and records of excessive medical expenses. You will need these and other documents to complete your applications.

5. Use the documents you've collected to complete required forms by the deadlines. Read directions carefully, and be consistent with your answers. Conflicting information on your application can delay your package. You may estimate your tax return information in order to meet deadlines. Estimate with care and send the actual data as soon as it becomes available.

6. Make copies of everything you submit and record the date of submission.

7. Receive and review for accuracy the documents you receive back from the FAFSA and PROFILE processors. Submit any revisions in writing directly to your financial aid office as soon as possible.

8. Receive and review your aid packages. Don't be afraid to call the financial aid office if you have questions. Try not to focus on only one aspect of your package, such as grant amounts, for example. Rather, look at the entire picture. Is one school asking you to borrow significantly more than others? Are budgets realistic? and so on. You might be able to negotiate your aid package if you have special circumstances that your school hasn't considered, or if you receive a better offer from a comparable school. The key to getting the fairest aid award possible is communicating with the financial aid office of the school your interested in.

9. Submit or update your student loan application based on your budget and financial aid at the school you will ultimately attend. Loan applications require processing time, so complete and submit them as early as possible.

10. Watch the bills from your school to make sure that all the funds you are counting on are credited to your account in a timely fashion. If there are any delays, call your school immediately. You are responsible for timely payment of your tuition bills.

CHAPTER *13*

Your Auto

Whether you have a car now, or just plan to get one in the future, you need to be aware that your car may be your biggest financial drain and the single largest waste of your money:

- The average price of a new car is well over $20,000 today.
- Most people will purchase 15 cars in their lifetime.
- At $20,000 each, those fifteen new cars will cost $300,000.
- If you finance them, your total cash spent on car payments will escalate to well over $400,000.

This absurd amount of cash wasted on cars can be drastically reduced. If you drive a new car, you can cut your automobile costs in half (or more) by driving a used car. Here's how it works:

New cars depreciate 50 percent in the first three years. That means that the value of the car actually decreases by 50 percent. In essence, you will make cash payments for three years, pay down the loan, and you still may not have any equity in the car. That is, the loan balance will likely exceed what the car is worth.

For example, suppose you bought an $18,000 car three years ago. You've been making payments of $260 every month for the past 36 months. The total of these payment is $9,360. But not all of that amount went toward paying down the principle balance. In fact, under the common financing "Rule of 78," most of the payment in the early years of an auto loan is payment of interest. In fact, in the first twelve months of a sixty-month "Rule of 78" loan, 35 percent of the entire interest will be paid. Payments in the later years are mostly applied to reducing the principle balance.

"Rule of 78" is a common type of loan amortization, whereby more interest is paid in the early years of the loan. Since most people keep their cars only three years, the finance company makes more interest income through this method. Watch out! Roughly a third of all banks and most finance companies use the rule of 78. Avoid it if at all possible. Ask for a simple interest loan, whereby you pay interest on the outstanding balance only.

In this example, assume that only $5,300 of the total was applied to reduce the principle balance. The remaining principle balance is now $12,700. That's the amount you would need today to pay your loan off. But, the car has depreciated 50 percent. That means that the market value is only $9,000. If you sold the car for its market value, after applying the $9,000 you got from selling it, you'd still owe $3,700 on the loan. You owe more on the car than it's worth.

Most people buy a new car every three years. Because of the heavy depreciation on the car in the first three years, their loan balance is always greater than the value of their car. They never have any equity, and yet they always have payments! So the $400,000 they spend in their lifetime on their cars goes straight to the car dealer and the bank. It's all cash out of their wallet, with no asset value to them.

If you buy a good-quality used car, you essentially let the first owner take the hit on the depreciation. In the fourth year, average depreciation slows way down to 20 percent. By the sixth year, depreciation is only 3 percent annually. By owning a car that's four years old or older, you have a financial advantage in several ways:

1. The price you pay is half or less compared to a new car.

2. The depreciation is much less than half. The market value of the car declines at a dramatically slower pace, and gives you the chance to build positive equity.

3. You save a significant amount of money on finance charges. Even if you finance a used car, the amount you finance (and thus, the cash spent on interest) is half that of a new car.

This is the concept that keeps millions of Americans in a spiral of auto debt. Once you understand this, you can free yourself from this trap and cut your car expenditures by half or more. The $400,000 you would otherwise spend on cars in your lifetime can be reduced to $200,000 or less. It's your choice. How important is it to you to drive a snazzy new car? Is it worth literally wasting $200,000 over your lifetime to have that pleasure?

Test your own car to determine where you are in the debt cycle:

1. Call your bank for the N.A.D.A. book value of your car. Give the year, make, model, specific options, and mileage. Place this amount in the blank in #1 below.

2. Ask your bank officer for the loan balance on your car. This is the amount necessary to pay your loan in full today. Place this amount in the blank in #2 below.

3. Subtract the N.A.D.A. book value from the loan balance. The difference is the positive or negative equity in your car.

Example:

1. N.A.D.A. Book Value: $_____
2. Loan Balance: minus   _____
3. Difference: Positive or Negative Equity: equals $_____

"N.A.D.A" stands for National Automobile Dealers Association. The N.A.D.A. guide for used car values is the definitive source for banks and lending institutions to determine how much a car is worth, and how much they will loan against it.

If the difference is a positive amount, then the value is greater than the debt, and you have positive equity in your car. That is, if you sold the car today at market value, you could pay off the loan and have money left over. You actually have some value in an asset. However, if the difference is a negative amount, then you owe more on the car than it's worth. If you sold the car today at market value, you would have to come up with extra cash to pay off the loan. This is a liability.

This concept is the very basis of financial success with automobiles. Most people never learn this and spend their entire life feeling helpless about their car debt.

Case Study Comparison

Marc bought a brand new compact for $22,000 and took out an 8 percent simple interest loan at the bank. His monthly payments were $446.17. After three years, his payments totaled $16,062, but only $12,137 was applied to the principle balance and $3,922 was paid in interest. He still owed $9,863 on the loan. At this time, the N.A.D.A. book value of the car was $11,500. As you can see, the $16,062 went to pay a lot of interest.

Conversely, Brooke shopped around for a good used car and paid $4,000 cash. Since it was five years old, most of the value would hold for a long time. Three years later, her car should be worth at least $2,500. So her cash outlay in three years is significantly lower than it would be for a new car.

HOW TO STAY OUT OF THE DEBT CYCLE

Your goal is very clear: Always own a car with positive equity. Your objective is to eventually pay the loan off completely and achieve 100 percent equity. You want to own the car outright with no loan attached to it, having a free and clear title. Ideally, you also want to continue to totally avoid debt on any car throughout your life. As you can see from the cost figures cited above, just avoiding car debt will save you at least $100,000 in finance charges in your lifetime.

You can do this by driving a good used car and keeping it for 150,000 to 200,000 miles. A durable car, purchased in good condition and well maintained during its use, should serve you reliably for a surprising number of miles. Your expenditures on regular, reasonable maintenance and normal repairs should not deplete your savings.

1. Start making extra payments on your car loan. Be sure to write "Principle Reduction Only" on the check and send a note specifying that the amount is to be applied to reducing the principle balance on the loan and that it is not a regular monthly payment. By making additional principle payments, you will pay the loan off sooner and pay less interest overall.

2. Be sure to protect the value of your asset by maintaining your car regularly and making repairs as soon as possible. Cars deteriorate when

they are neglected. Problems that are ignored never go away; they only become bigger and more expensive.

3. Once you've paid off the debt, continue to make regular "payments" to your savings. This cache will serve as a fund to be used to pay cash for your next car purchase. Remember, you will have cash proceeds from the sale of your current car that can also be applied to the purchase of the new car. Using this system will ensure that you never have to finance a car again.

HOW TO BUY A GOOD USED CAR

Saving money on cars requires that you start with a good, dependable car. When you buy a used car, consult resources such as *Consumer Reports* in your library or bookstore for makes and models with the highest ratings for dependability and repairs. Do your homework and decide what you want to buy before you begin your car search.

1. Pick two or three models to shop for specifically. Your choices will be governed by the type of vehicle you need and how you use it. Check the published used car resources carefully for recall histories, repair histories, performance ratings, and longevity ratings. Choose cars that rank high among these for sustaining value.

2. Narrow your search down to an age range that is within your budget. Start at age three in order to avoid the heavy depreciation. Many cars are built to last and are very good values if they've been taken care of.

3. Limit the mileage to 15,000 miles per year. Excessive mileage is often a sign of overuse or abuse. Screen cars for low mileage.

4. Look only at cars that fit these criteria. You can eliminate a lot of wasted time by asking lots of questions on the phone.

5. Scrutinize the quality of the car extremely carefully before buying it. Many good books are available in the library or bookstore to lead you through this process. Among the key points to consider:

   • Has the oil been changed every 3,000 miles?
   • Does the owner have all service records?
   • Does it need any repairs?
   • Why are they selling it?

6. Have a mechanic thoroughly inspect the car before you buy it. This should cost only $50–$75 and could alleviate the huge expense and heartache of buying a bad car.

Finding a great used car at a good price may take awhile. But it can be done. Let your friends and relatives know that you're in the market for a dependable used car. Sometimes the best deals come through friends who are about to trade in for a new car. Your patience and diligence may save you thousands of dollars each year.

> Denice felt particularly intimidated by the process of shopping for a used car. She recommends having a knowledgeable male friend or family member along to dispel the "easy target" notion. "If I'm going to a used car lot, I want to let the salesman know that I'm not going to be coerced. So I tell them right up front that I've studied car values and I'm getting outside advice. Bringing my brother helps send the message that I'm serious."

WHAT ABOUT LEASING?

With the drastic rise in new car prices in recent years, manufacturers and dealers have been promoting leasing as a more affordable option. For a select few, it may well be. But for the majority of us, leasing entails significant financial risk that may not be apparent on the front end. That's when you're less likely to scrutinize the fine print and more inclined to sign up in a flurry of emotion. Before you obligate yourself to a long contract, carefully consider these aspects of leasing:

- Most leases charge a hefty premium at the end if you exceed the mileage limits. For example, suppose your five-year lease charges $0.15 for each mile in excess of 12,000 miles per year. You actually drove it 82,500 miles, or an average of 16,500 miles per year. Your excess mileage charge at the end of the lease would be $3,375. This is what you must come up with in cash to turn your lease car in!

- Most leases charge a discretionary amount for excessive wear and tear. You are completely at their mercy. They alone reserve the right to determine what "excessive" means, as well as the amount they charge.

- If you must end the lease early, severe financial penalties are imposed. This is all detailed in the fine print of the lease agreement you signed.

- When you finish all your obligations under the lease, you own nothing. Remember, your lease is only a contract that entitles you to use the car for a specified term at a specified price. You pay dearly for this privilege and end up owning nothing. For this reason, if you plan to keep the car for longer than three years, you are generally better off buying rather than leasing.

However, to be perfectly fair, there are certain advantages to leasing for a select group of people:

- If you're not at all concerned about the overall financial benefits of a car purchase, you can sometimes lease a car for a lower monthly payment.

- Leasing may be attractive if your up-front lease costs are less than the down payment on a car you purchase. (But you'll pay for it in the long run.)

- Some "full maintenance" leases offer service as a part of the lease package. Be careful; they may stipulate specific locations and procedures.

More Ways to Lower Your Car Expenses

If you choose only one thing to lower your car costs, it should unquestionably be changing your oil and oil filter every three thousand miles. Far and away, this is the single most important thing you can do. Keeping your engine clean and lubricated will dramatically extend the life of your car and minimize engine problems. Additionally, you will save money if you:

- Familiarize yourself with the maintenance schedule in the owner's manual and follow it. Most repairs can be eliminated or reduced with proper maintenance or earlier detection.

- Be alert for changes in your car's performance. They are red flags to early detection of problems.

- Watch your indicator gauges and lights. They will alert you to changes in your car's performance that may need attention. When indicators change, stop at a garage and ask what it might mean.

- Get a second opinion if you still have questions or feel uncomfortable.

- Attend to small problems immediately. Problems never go away. They always grow bigger and more expensive.

- Change all fluids and filters regularly. A good quick oil change facility will include this inspection at no charge or for a nominal fee.

- Keep track of your gas mileage. A drop may be an early sign of a problem.

- These things put a heavy burden on your engine and wear it out quicker:

  - Stop and go driving, as in the city
  - Driving with one foot resting on the brake or clutch
  - Cold starts and short trips
  - Pulling heavy loads, especially trailers
  - Driving on dusty roads

HOW TO FIND A GOOD, TRUSTWORTHY MECHANIC

Not all mechanics are out to rip you off. Really. Surprising as it sounds, the good ones are out there; it just takes an effort to find them. A few secrets will help you zero in on the best mechanics and assure that you get great service at a reasonable cost.

Ask your family, friends, and coworkers for their recommendations. Ask them who they liked and who they didn't like. Reputation by word of mouth is extremely powerful and accurate.

Ask the reputable used car dealers in your area whom they use for repairs on their inventory. The vast majority of used cars on a lot have been repaired in some way by a mechanic for the dealer's inventory. Used car dealers use repair shops that they know and trust. And you can bet that they are not being overcharged. Ask whom they use, and if they might call the mechanic to refer you. This sends a powerful message to their professional peers: "Treat this person right."

Consider testing the shop's work with a small repair or maintenance job first. Speak to the owner or manager directly if at all possible. Ask them for a dozen business cards. Maria, 22, has found a great way to get their attention. "I tell them that if I'm satisfied with their work, I have dozens of friends who are eager to find a good mechanic with reasonable rates. I'd love to take a stack of his business cards and pass them out."

Before you leave your car for repairs, be sure to:

1. Describe your car's symptoms only. Take the mechanic for a test drive to demonstrate the problem. Let the mechanic diagnose the illness.

2. Get a written estimate of specific repairs and costs. On the original work order, authorize only the estimated repairs. Specify in writing that any repair exceeding that amount must be authorized by you.

3. Be aware of how they treat you. Do they listen to you? Do they answer your questions fully? Do they treat you with respect? If not, leave. Go somewhere else.

4. Always feel free to get a second opinion. In the case of major repairs, this is always advisable.

5. Before you pay for your repairs, take the mechanic for another test drive to demonstrate that the problem is solved. It is much easier to resolve a dispute before you pay.

Avoid These Car Repair Rip-Offs

According to a 1993 Department of Transportation study, an astonishing 40 percent of auto repair costs are unnecessary! Rip-offs are perpetrated in as many ways as you can imagine. The most common are:

Phantom Repairs

You may be charged for repairs that were never made. Example: You are charged for a new alternator when they replaced only an inexpensive alternator belt. Solution: Always ask to see the old parts when you sign the work order. This puts them on notice that you aren't naive.

Make-Work Repairs

You may be charged for a full job when only a small repair would have been sufficient. Example: They do a full brake job when only a simple replacement of pads was necessary. Solution: When they diagnose the problem, ask them to show you and explain in detail. Ask if a less expensive solution is possible. If you are suspicious, get a second opinion.

Charges for Repairs That Should Be Free

You may be charged for repairs that are covered under your warranty. Solution: Familiarize yourself with your warranty before you drop your car off. Ask the dealer what's covered.

Lowball Prices

Shops often "lure" new customers in with great advertised specials on regular maintenance jobs, then try to sell you on more lucrative repairs while your car is there. Solution: If you feel pressured by them in this tactic, be wary. Be sure to take your time and get a second opinion.

In any case, remember that you are the customer and that they are in business to meet your needs. Be inquisitive. Ask questions. Expect respect from them. Above all, they are there to serve you. If it feels like they are intimidating you, walk away. Go elsewhere.

COMMONLY ASKED QUESTIONS

How much can I afford?

Of course, every car is different, but the average cost of running a new car is $6,000 per year. That includes gas, oil, maintenance, insurance, depreciation, interest, tires, and licenses. That amount is in addition to the initial purchase price. A used car may be a lot less than that, if it is dependable and requires little repair.

I know a used car is cheaper, but I really, really want a new car. Any advice?

Before you buy, find out what kind of a depreciation hit you're likely to take in the first three years. Some models depreciate much more rapidly than others. Look up the N.A.D.A. average retail price for the exact same car (or as close as you can get) that was new three years ago. Compare that with the retail price today. This is the amount that you're likely to lose in the next three years. Are you prepared to take that hit?

Should I buy an extended warranty?

Perhaps. But first, be sure you know what you're buying. According to the Federal Trade Commission, what is commonly referred to as an extended warranty is actually a service contract, as defined by federal law. Check the standard warranty and compare for duplicate coverages.

How can I ensure that the mileage hasn't been rolled back on a used car before I buy it?

Although rolling back mileage is illegal, it is a common practice. To protect yourself, take a close look at the driver's side upholstery, door handles, floorboards, and steering wheel for signs of mileage that belie the odometer. Does it look like it's been driven harder than it says? It probably has. Or, try contacting the previous owner to discuss it. Old service records may document mileage that exceeds the odometer reading. If you can't locate the records themselves, try the garage where it was serviced. In the end, if you have suspicions, it's safer to pass than to take the chance.

CHAPTER 14

Housing

According to the Census Bureau, the average American spends about 28 percent of his or her income on housing. Quite a chunk, especially when you tally that up for a year, five years, ten years. Up until the end of World War II, the majority of Americans lived in housing owned by others. Today, only about 36 percent rent rather than own. Renting is increasingly the first choice for people under thirty.

Pros of Renting

- The lifestyle is simpler. Fewer hassles, fewer headaches. This is especially attractive if you travel.

- Renting gives you more flexibility than owning. You can locate somewhere temporarily and move more easily.

- You don't need a large down payment to get into most rental units. However, you probably will need some type of small deposit (more on that later).

- Expenses are lower. Repairs and maintenance are typically the landlord's responsibility.

- You avoid unexpected cash outlays. No dipping into savings to replace the leaky roof.

- Renting often allows you to save money for investments or for a down payment for a house.

Cons of Renting

- Rentals usually offer less space than your own home might.

- Noise and privacy may be issues.

- You build no equity and take no tax deductions.

- You may not be able to customize it to suit your tastes and lifestyle.

- Renting can't give you that "proud homeowner" feeling.

BEFORE YOU SIGN THAT LEASE

Leases are contracts. They are legal documents that are binding. You want to read them very carefully, making sure that you can fulfill every last one of the obligations. They are not easy to get out of and are reliably upheld in a court of law. In addition to reading the lease terms carefully, make sure you can answer these questions to your satisfaction before signing it:

- What happens if you wish to move before your lease term ends? Can you cancel the lease with notice, or are you obligated to pay the remaining rent no matter what?

- Does the lease allow for an assignment or sublease to fulfill the lease term? (Note: An assignment is preferable. In a sublease, you remain ultimately responsible for payment.)

- Does the landlord reserve the right to increase rents or will rents be fixed for the lease term?

- Are utilities included in the monthly rent? If not, is each unit metered individually?

- What happens if you paint or wallpaper? Add shelves?

You can learn a lot about a place by talking to the people who live there. Now is the time to take a few minutes to speak with your future neighbors to get their input. You'll want to know what it's really like, especially the negatives. Just how bad is it? These folks can tell you:

- Are there reports of crime or violence?

- Do they feel safe walking outside to and from their car at night? Are public areas well lighted?

- Is the security reliable? Does anyone patrol periodically?

- Who do you call if something seems suspicious or scary?

- Does the landlord return phone calls?

- Does management respond quickly and professionally to requests for maintenance or repairs?

- Are there any bug problems? Noise problems?

- Is parking adequate?

- Ask one final catch-all question: What are the biggest negatives of living there?

WHAT IS YOUR DEPOSIT FOR?

You don't necessarily have to kiss your deposit good-bye the moment you hand it over. If you ask enough questions up-front and make sure that the lease clearly defines the deposit terms, chances are you can get the deposit back after you comply with the terms. Find out exactly what type of deposit it is and what the restrictions are. Here are the most typical kinds of deposits.

Damage Deposits

Damage may be defined as physical damage to property or economic damage to the landlord by breaking the lease. Physical damage usually exceeds normal wear and tear, but is usually at the discretion of the manager. If they are sticklers, even nail holes may be deemed damage for which they withhold deposits. Before you move in, survey the unit and document the condition of any questionable items. You may even want to take photos. Ask the leasing agent to attach a copy of your documentation to the lease itself for future reference.

Security Deposits

Security deposits often act just like damage deposits with one modification. They may stipulate that you are not eligible for a refund unless you fulfill the term of the lease.

Cleaning Deposits

Usually not refundable, cleaning deposits are held for cleaning expenses incurred after you move out. Even if you leave the place spotless, they may impose charges for such services as carpet cleaning and blind cleaning. Most often, it is nearly impossible to do these yourself to their satisfaction.

PROS AND CONS OF OWNING A HOME

Not surprisingly, the list of pros and cons for owning a home is exactly the opposite of the list for renting. The initial costs and ongoing costs are much higher than renting. It is important to understand that the financial obligations of home ownership are much more variable and even unpredictable. Many experts advise that if you buy, you should plan to stay for at least four years in order to recoup your initial outlay and begin to build real equity.

IS HOUSING A GOOD INVESTMENT?

According to the National Association of Realtors, the median price of an existing home has increased dramatically over the years, suggesting an investment return due to appreciation:

1970	$23,000
1980	$62,200
1990	$95,500

Compared to the Consumer Price Index or CPI (an economic indicator of inflation), the average national increase in housing prices of existing homes often outpaces inflation, but may not keep pace long term. For the decade ending in 1990:

Year	CPI Increase	Sales Price Increase
1981	10.3	6.7
1982	6.2	2.1
1983	3.2	3.7
1984	4.3	2.9
1985	3.6	4.2
1986	1.9	6.4
1987	3.6	6.9
1988	4.1	4.0
1989	4.8	2.6
1990	5.4	2.6
Average	4.7	4.2

As an investment, housing varies drastically from one neighborhood to another and from one house to another. Do research in your market before you jump into it.

WHAT CAN YOU AFFORD TO BUY?

As a general rule, lenders will consider a home that costs up to two and a half times your annual income. They also impose certain qualifying tests, ratios, and credit requirements. The process can be long and complicated, but with some fundamental knowledge, you can take charge.

The Down Payment

Most lenders require a minimum of 10 percent cash down payment at closing. The balance can be financed through a mortgage.

Closing Costs

Most professionals estimate that an additional 7 percent of the amount of the purchase will be tacked on at closing for miscellaneous closing costs, such as commissions, points, fees, inspections, and the like. (Be sure to go over each one of these in detail before dishing out your cash. Mistakes are often made on the closing statement.)

Qualifying Ratios

Your mortgage payment, property taxes and homeowners insurance should not exceed 28 percent of your total income. If you pass that test, you must also show that the total of all your proposed monthly payment such as mortgage expenses, credit cards, and student loans will not exceed 36 percent of your total income. If your debt payments are too high, you may be able to pay them off in order to qualify.

Other Costs

After paying the initial acquisition costs of your home, the monthly financial obligations are much higher than renting. In addition to your monthly mortgage payment, carefully consider these expenses:

- Utilities
- Property taxes
- Property insurance
- Maintenance and repairs
- Services, such as trash pickup, lawn care, and snow removal
- Possible assessments for streets, sidewalks, and sewers

ABSOLUTELY DON'T MISS THIS!

When you get serious about buying a home, you can negotiate the best price, shop for the best mortgage, pay attention to all the details, and still miss the forest for the trees. You can end up with a deal that costs you twice as much and saps many thousands of dollars in unnecessary interest expense. You can avoid this trap altogether. And the concept is simple.

Most Americans mortgage their home over the standard 30 years. Let's assume that you finance $95,000 on your first home at 8.5 percent interest over thirty years (360 monthly payments). Look at how that payment breaks down into principle and interest, as well as the total of those payments over the entire term:

Monthly payment:	$730.47
× Total # of payments	× 360
= Total paid	$262,969

Over the entire term of the mortgage, you will have paid $262,969 for the $95,000 principal that you financed. That means that over the 30 years, you paid $167,969 in interest:

Total paid	$262,969
Less: Principal amount	– 95,000
= Interest paid	$167,969

By shortening the life of your mortgage, you can shave the interest amount by well over $120,000! Here's what your payments and the related principle and interest look like over ten and 15 years for the same $95,000 financed at 8.5 percent:

	@ 30 years	@ 15 years	@ 10 years
Monthly payment	$730.47	$935.51	$1177.87
× Total # of payments	× 360	× 180	× 120
= Total paid	$262,969	$168,392	$141,344
Less: Principal amount	– 95,000	– 95,000	– 95,000
= Interest paid	$167,969	$73,392	$46,344

Note that the monthly payment is larger for the shorter term mortgages. If you can afford the higher payments, you'll save $121,625 by financing your home over ten years instead of 30 years.

So why is a 30-year mortgage standard in America today? Simply because our economy is built on the theory of credit—buy now, pay later. Mortgage interest is big business, and mortgage companies make a lot of money at the expense of the consumer. But you can win this game by being smart and using credit wisely.

CHAPTER 15

Taxes

The IRS processes over 115 million returns each year, collecting almost 500 billion dollars from individual taxpayers. The average American works over 128 days—until May 8—to pay his individual federal, state, and local taxes.

But it hasn't always been this way. Most Americans didn't even file a tax return, much less pay taxes before 1940. Before that, the gross annual income required to file a return was $5,000. The average citizen just didn't make that much. And from 1895 to 1913, the Supreme Court deemed income taxes unconstitutional.

WITHHOLDING

The IRS began withholding taxes from wages in 1943 in order to regulate the flow of cash into the Treasury. When you begin a new job, your withholdings are determined by completing IRS Form W-4. As you earn a salary, a percentage is withheld each pay period. These withholdings serve as a prepayment of your tax bill. For more information, ask the IRS office near you for their Publication 919 *Is My Withholding Correct?*

If you are self-employed, you must pay estimated taxes quarterly if you will owe at least $500 on income not subject to withholding. These requirements are outlined in IRS Publication 505 Tax Withholding and Estimated Tax. Payment dates are April 15, June 15, September 15, and January 15. The total of all estimated tax payments must be at least 90 percent of the actual tax due, or severe penalties may be imposed.

FILING A TAX RETURN

Your tax return is required by law to be postmarked by midnight on April 15. If you need additional time, you may apply for an automatic extension to August 15 by mailing IRS Form 4868 "Application for Automatic Extension of Time to File U.S. Individual Income Tax Return." When you file your return, you are actually settling your tax bill for the past year. The IRS provides a Forms and Instructions booklet to guide you through the system.

IRS PUBLICATIONS

Most taxpayers receive a packet from the IRS with an instruction book and the related forms. Or, you can get the forms and schedules you need from the regional IRS office near you or by calling them at (800) 829-3676. Local post offices, libraries, and banks often stock the basic forms you may need. A complete list of IRS publications is available by requesting Publication 17 *Your Federal Income Tax*. Other helpful publications are:

> 502 *Medical and Dental Expenses*
> 503 *Child and Dependent Care Expenses*
> 504 *Divorced or Separated Individuals*
> 505 *Tax Withholding and Estimated Tax*
> 521 *Moving Expenses*
> 525 *Taxable and Nontaxable Income*
> 529 *Miscellaneous Deductions*
> 530 *Tax Information for First-Time Homebuyers*
> 547 *Nonbusiness Disasters, Casualties, and Thefts*
> 550 *Investment Income and Expenses*
> 552 *Record Keeping for Individuals*
> 910 *Guide to Free Tax Services*

THE TAX STRUCTURE

The United States operates under a *progressive* tax structure, which means that the more you earn, the higher your tax rate. Tax rates are divided into five tiers, or tax brackets. As of this writing, the first bracket is taxed at 15 percent, the next at 28 percent, the third at 31 percent, the fourth at 36 percent, and the highest at 39.6 percent. A single taxpayer with taxable income of $70,000 pays $16,835.50 in taxes:

	15% of the first	$24,000 =		$3,600.00
plus:	28% of the next	$34,150 =		$9,562.00
plus:	31% of the last	$11,850 =		$3,673.50
	Total income:	$70,000	Total tax:	$16,835.50

TAX PLANNING

It is perfectly legal, moral, and desirable to reduce your tax bill by planning ahead and utilizing some basic tax reduction strategies. Not all strategies will work for everyone. At this point it is highly advisable to seek the advice of a trusted professional. The following summary will give you just enough information to ask meaningful questions and get advice tailored to your individual tax situation. Don't despair if you aren't clear about all the terms and definitions used.

Miscellaneous Itemized Deductions

Certain expenses you pay in a given tax year may be deductible. Some may be subject to specific minimums. For example, medical expenses that exceed 7.5 percent of your adjusted gross income could qualify. Other potential deductions include subscriptions to medical journals, continuing education courses that relate to your current job, union and professional dues, certain job-hunting expenses, investment management fees, and tax preparation fees, among others.

Tax-Free Investments

Interest paid on certain municipal bonds sold by state or local governments is not subject to federal taxes. Ever.

Tax-Deferred Investments

Since you don't have the use of the earnings on certain investments, you don't have to pay taxes until you withdraw the funds. This category includes certain qualified retirement plans such as 401(k) and 403(b) as well as IRAs and certain annuities.

Flexible Spending Plans

Under these plans, a fixed dollar amount is excluded from your salary to pay medical and dependent care expenses. The amount excluded is also excluded when calculating your income for tax purposes.

Borrowing for Investment

Interest paid on qualifying loans taken out to finance investments is tax deductible. Be sure to work with a professional. Not just any loan qualifies. For more information, see IRS publication 550, *Investment + Income and Expenses.*

Home Equity Loans

Interest paid on qualifying home equity loans, is tax deductible. The interest paid on your credit cards, student loans, and consumer debt is not. If possible, transfer nondeductible debt to a home equity loan.

Giving to Charity

When something you own (common stocks, for example) appreciates or increases in value, you may end up owing taxes. You could avoid the tax bill by donating the appreciated property to charity. The rules are stringent and you probably need professional advice before doing this.

HELP!

Professional tax advisors and preparers come in all shapes and sizes. To help you navigate the maze, the following chart offers an introduction:

Category	Typical Fees	Services and Additional Information
Tax Preparers	$100 or less	• Usually prepare uncomplicated returns • Experience and skills not certified • Don't give advice and don't represent you to IRS
Enrolled Agents	$100–300	• Five years of IRS audit experience • Certified by the Treasury Department • May represent you to IRS
Certified Public Accountants	$500–2,500	• Not all are tax specialists • Can advise you throughout year • Can represent you to IRS
Tax Attorneys	$1,000 +	• Do not prepare returns • Offer tax and legal advice can represent you to IRS and courts

How do you decide which one is best for you? Start looking for tax help before you really need it. Don't wait until March to begin your search. Interview at least one advisor in each category to determine what level of service you need. If you already know what type of help you need, then interview several in that category to find one who listens and understands what your objectives are. Don't forget to ask for professional references, and really check them out.

AVOID THESE COMMON TAX MISTAKES

Not Getting Professional Tax Planning Advice
All of the preceding tax reduction strategies work for some people. You won't know what they can do for you unless you get knowledgeable guidance. And seek advice early. You run the risk of wasting an entire year and paying hundreds or thousands more in taxes if you procrastinate.

Not Following Through
Once you get the advice, don't wait. Go out and implement the strategies right away.

Not Keeping Receipts
Many people let valuable deductions float away by ignoring or losing simple receipts. Once you know what to keep, establish a habit of saving receipts in a specific section of your wallet. Then, periodically, file them away for tax preparation time.

Not Keeping Copies and Accurate Records
Make copies of every income tax return you file. Be sure to check last year's return for carry forward items to the current year. Even one overlooked item can cost you thousands in overpaid taxes.

Not Withholding Enough
If you consistently get a big refund every year, you are overpaying your withholding. This is the same as giving the government a tax-free loan of your hard-earned money. Instead, decrease your withholdings and invest the additional proceeds in an interest-earning asset, for example, your savings account.

$ECTION 4
Your Financial Future

CHAPTER 16

Earning Potential of Popular Career Paths

It can be daunting, indeed. How can you possibly decide what major to declare when you have no earthly idea what you want to do? "Undecided" seems like the safest bet for now. The problem with that approach is that it's easy to ignore the question and slide too long without giving it much thought. Then, when you have to decide for real, you probably haven't explored the possibilities and you're still undecided. According to one senior at a large university in the southwest:

> "I went 'undecided' until I was a junior. Then I had to declare, and I didn't know what I wanted. If I had it to do over, I'd think about it more seriously as a sophomore. As it turned out, I wasted too much time and ended up missing my graduation by a semester."

Majors can easily be changed if you're not deep into the required courses. About 70 percent of all college students change their majors two or three times before their junior year. So go ahead and declare a major that seems to appeal to you most. That way, you can meet other students and professors who can help you discover more about the field. Ask about jobs, typical working environments, typical days in certain jobs, and the kinds of people who hold those jobs.

Does it sound like the area of your choice involves activities you would enjoy? That's really the bottom line. Life's way too short to spend five or even six days a week doing a job you dislike. But many, many people do exactly that. By giving it a little thought now, you can change the direction of the rest of your life. Consider these areas of interest, as described in the U.S. Department of Labor's *Guide for Occupational Exploration:*

Artistic

Do you like to express your feelings or ideas creatively?
Are you inclined to write or perform?

Scientific

Are you interested in discovering, collecting, and analyzing information?
Do you enjoy applying research findings to solving problems?
Are you intrigued with life sciences, natural sciences, or medicine?

Plants and Animals

Do you love being outdoors?
Do you like physical work?

Protective

Do you feel challenged by protecting people and property?
Is having authority important to you?

Mechanical

Is a hands-on project most satisfying to you?
Are you good at applying mechanical principles to practical situations?

Industrial

Are you looking for an organized environment, with lots of order?
Do you like to work with machines instead of people?

Business Detail

Does an office job appeal to you?
Do you enjoy details?

Selling

Are you persuasive with others?
Do you really like working with other people?

Accommodating

Do you have an interest in helping others?
Do you like one-on-one interaction with others?

Humanitarian

Do you care deeply about the welfare of others?
Do you want to help with others' mental, spiritual, social, physical, or vocational needs?

Leading and Influencing

Do you have high level verbal or numerical abilities?
Are you interested in a position of responsibility and authority?

Physical Performing

Are you gifted in athletics or performing?
Do you like to perform for an audience?

This is just a teaser to help you get in touch with your true areas of interest. Your challenge is to focus on your interests, values, strengths, and abilities to uncover a wide range of choices and select a field that is suited to you. There are lots of resources out there to help you. Your school's career counseling cervices are a vastly underutilized wealth of information to help you sort it through.

Sources of Career Information

Resources are as close as your fingertips and probably no further than the other side of campus. Most all of the information is free, just for the asking. And people love to help by offering their experiences and advice.

Personal Contacts

We often overlook some of the most valuable sources of real-life information that are right in front of us: our friends and family. They can tell you what they've experienced, as well as what they'd do if they had it to do over again. Sometimes the most valuable information is in someone else's mistakes. Network with them. If they can't answer your questions, chances are they know someone who does. Networking is especially helpful to get information that's more subjective, such as what's good and bad about a job and how to advance in the field.

Counselors

Counselors are trained to help you discover your strengths and weaknesses and guide you through an evaluation of your values and goals. By administering interest inventories and aptitude tests, counselors will help you interpret the results and explore your options. Counselors will not tell you what to do. That's up to you to decide. Counselors may also be able to give you insights into entry requirements, costs for training, and the job outlook in your areas of interest.

You can find vocational counselors in:

- College career planning and placement offices
- Vocational rehabilitation agencies
- Counseling services offered by community organizations
- Private counseling agencies
- State employment service offices affiliated with the U.S. Employment Service

Career Centers

Far too many students put off using the career center until it is too late to fully benefit from its services. A complete career resource library is stocked with hundreds of publications and up-to-date reports in all areas of interest. Career centers also offer individual counseling, group discussions, guest speakers, field trips, and career days. You can visit without an appointment, and the staff is ready and able to lead you through your exploration.

Career Centers have taken advantage of sophisticated technologies to enhance your search and provide you with timely information. Computerized career exploration software such as "Discover" will help you uncover exciting career fields that match your interests. Career center computers are now linked to the worldwide web job listing services. These services are offered privately for hundreds of dollars, but if you're a student, they're yours free. "We offer all students a wealth of information and we're here exclusively to help them in their career search. Unfortunately, only a fraction of the student population explores these resources," reports a career counselor at a large university.

Internet Networks and Resources

If you have access to the Internet, you can enter a world of approximately 20,000 computer networks, each containing millions of computer systems and users. You can find an almost incalculable amount of information on almost any subject imaginable.

The World Wide Web is one of the fastest growing and easiest to use parts of the Internet. Through your Internet server (e.g., America Online) try keyword searches for job-related topics such as "Jobnet." Or, click on the Web Crawler to select topics of interest, including "Jobnet." Specific Web sites of interest in your explorations include:

Jobnet
  Web page that links to job-related resources all over the Internet
  To access, type http://www.jobweb.org.

CareerMosaic
   For information about employers, companies and job opportunities
   To access, type http://www.careermosaic.com/cm/.

Résumé Server
   To post your resume for viewing and to view others' résumés online
   To access, type http://www. resumesnet. com.

Additional job-related resources on the Internet are available through other web sites, Gopher servers, Usenet newsgroups, and mailing list servers. It may be helpful to consult The Internet Yellow Pages. Just plug in and log on. You don't need to be an expert to use it.

DEGREES AWARDED AND STARTING SALARIES

A recent salary survey of 359 college career planning and placement offices across the United States yielded some tremendously enlightening results. New college graduates can expect a positive job market with significant increases in starting salaries for the right professions. The survey encompassed offers and salaries to 4,874 new graduates:

Total offers to bachelor's nontechnical degrees	2,303	47.3%
Total offers to bachelor's technical degrees	2,571	52.7%

Job offers to these candidates were generally categorized as follows:

Services employers	49.4%
Manufacturing employers	36.0%
Government/nonprofit employers	14.6%

Below is a summary of these job offers. The listing is segmented into non-technical Bachelors degrees and technical bachelor's degrees. Each segment is further divided into services, manufacturing, and nonprofit/government employers.

Bachelor's Nontechnical Degrees

Services Employers	# of Offers	% of Total	Average Salary
Public Accounting	448	9.19	$29,707
Advertising	17	.35	$20,765
Architectural Services	1	.02	$22,000
Banking (commercial)	84	1.72	$24,246
Banking (investment)	30	.62	$29,909
Communication Services	63	1.29	$25,269
Computer Software/Data Processing	79	1.62	$29,611
Consulting Services	98	2.01	$31,168
Engineering/Surveying	4	.08	$27,750
Environmental/Waste Management	2	.04	$21,625
Finance	142	2.91	$26,207
Hospitality (Recreation/Fast Food)	31	.64	$22,960
Hospitality (Hotel/Restaurant)	66	1.35	$24,794
Insurance	97	1.99	$27,701
Legal Services	6	.12	$20,500
Merchandising	192	3.94	$24,229
Personnel Supply Services	17	.35	$22,623
Protective Services	3	.06	$18,667
Publishing	28	.57	$20,836
Real Estate	14	.29	$25,393
Research Organizations	16	.33	$26,894
Transportation	37	.76	$25,106
Utilities	10	.21	$27,910
Other service employers	62	1.27	$23,795
Total	1,547		

Manufacturing Employers	# of Offers	% of Total	Average Salary
Aerospace	16	.33	$31,707
Agribusiness & Products	12	.25	$28,642
Building Materials and Construction	14	.29	$28,514
Automotive and Mechanical	26	.53	$28,753
Chemicals and Allied Products	14	.29	$29,553
Pharmaceuticals	15	.31	$34,800
Computers/Business Equipment	23	.47	$30,244
Electrical/Electronics	28	.57	$28,958
Food & Beverage	51	1.05	$28,890
Household & Personal Care	11	.23	$28,982
Metals and Metal Products	6	.12	$25,771
Packaging & Allied Products	1	.02	$34,000
Paper & Wood Products	16	.33	$29,081
Petroleum	11	.23	$27,350
Printing	9	.18	$27,411
Rubber Products	1	.02	$16,640
Scientific/Industrial Measuring Instruments	5	.10	$30,020
Stone, Clay, Glass, & Concrete	1	.02	$10,500
Textiles & Apparel	10	.21	$28,479
Widely Diversified	23	.47	$30,226
Total	293		

Nonprofit/Gov't	# of Offers	% of Total	Average Salary
Education	248	5.09	$22,063
Federal Government	44	.90	$25,256
Hospitals	16	.33	$21,670

Health Services	26	.53	$22,418
Local/State Government	76	1.56	$23,629
Membership/Religious	14	.29	$18,523
Museums/Cultural	5	.10	$19,590
Social Services	31	.64	$20,346
Other Nonprofit Employers	9	.18	$21,913
Total	469		

Bachelor's Technical Degrees

Services Employers	# of Offers	% of Total	Average Salary
Public Accounting	6	.12	$34,434
Advertising	2	.04	$22,500
Architectural Services	18	.37	$32,111
Banking (commercial)	8	.16	$31,749
Banking (investment)	5	.10	$33,520
Communication Services	57	1.17	$35,272
Computer Software/Data Processing	224	4.6	$35,077
Consulting Services	221	4.53	$34,532
Engineering/Surveying	121	2.48	$34,108
Environmental/Waste Management	11	.23	$29,575
Finance	19	.39	$31,842
Hospitality (Recreation/Fast Food)	4	08	$21,855
Hospitality (Hotel/Restaurant)	1	.02	$25,000
Insurance	24	.49	$31,279
Legal Services	2	.04	$22,500
Merchandising	49	1.0	$42,702
Personnel Supply Services	2	.04	$22,500
Protective Services	1	.02	$20,000

Publishing	3	.06	$23,000
Real Estate	1	.02	$32,000
Research Organizations	8	.16	$31,855
Transportation	25	.51	$32,038
Utilities	20	.41	$34,702
Other Service Employers	28	.57	$31,550
Total	860		

Manufacturing Employers	# of Offers	% of Total	Average Salary
Aerospace	104	2.13	$36,040
Agribusiness and Products	53	1.08	$34,849
Building Materials and Construction	91	1.87	$32,318
Automotive and Mechanical	201	4.12	$37,804
Chemicals and Allied Products	150	3.08	$41,581
Pharmaceuticals	9	.18	$36,864
Computers/Business Equipment	180	3.69	$37,763
Electrical/Electronics	256	5.25	$37,441
Food & Beverage	73	1.5	$36,808
Household and Personal Care	19	.39	$41,755
Metals and Metal Products	52	1.07	$36,024
Mining	19	.39	$36,722
Packaging and Allied Products	7	.14	$37,229
Paper and Wood Products	33	.68	$37,741
Petroleum	109	2.24	$40,839
Printing	4	.08	$32,000
Rubber Products	9	.18	$39,940
Scientific/Industrial Measuring Instruments	12	.25	$34,269
Stone, Clay, Glass, & Concrete	5	.10	$38,380

Textiles & Apparel	6	.12	$34,250
Widely Diversified	77	1.58	$37,211
Total	1,469		

Nonprofit/Gov't	# of Offers	% of Total	Average Salary
Education	28	.57	$25,650
Federal Government	54	1.10	$28,404
Hospitals	86	1.76	$31,934
Health Services	32	.66	$32,801
Local/State Government	34	.70	$26,399
Membership/Religious	1	.02	$30,000
Museums/Cultural	2	.04	$13,720
Social Services	4	.08	$20,500
Other Nonprofit Employers	1	.02	$26,000
Total	242		

Total offers to Bachelor's Degree Candidates by Employers: 4,880

Source: Salary Survey, March 1996, National Association of Colleges and Employer 62 Highland Avenue, Bethlehem, PA 18017

TOMORROW'S JOBS AND JOB GROWTH

Making informed career decisions requires consideration of jobs and opportunities in the future. To help guide your career plans, the Bureau of Labor Statistics projects industry and occupational employment. Highlights of their most recently published projections for job growth through the year 2005 include:*

- A slowdown in employment growth is expected

- Service-producing industries will account for most new jobs

- The goods-producing sector will decline

- The fastest-growing occupations are in computer technology and health services

- Education and training affect job opportunities

- Jobs requiring the most education and training will be the fastest growing and highest paying

- Jobs requiring the least education and training will provide the most openings, but offer the lowest pay

- The labor force will continue to grow faster than the population

- Women will continue to comprise an increasing share of the labor force

- The labor force will become increasingly diverse

The report also projects specific job growth. Twenty occupations will account for half of all job growth from 1994–2005. These twenty occupations have the largest numerical increase in employment:

Job Type	# of New Jobs
Cashiers	560,000
Janitors and Cleaners	560,000
Salespersons, Retail	520,000
Waiters and Waitresses	490,000
Registered Nurses	480,000
General Managers and Top Executives	470,000
Systems Analysts	450,000
Home Health Aides	430,000
Guards	420,000
Nursing aides and attendants	390,000
Teachers, secondary school	390,000
Marketing and sales supervisors	380,000
Teacher aides and assistants	370,000

Receptionists and clerks	325,000
Truck drivers	280,000
Secretaries (except legal/medical)	275,000
Clerical supervisors	260,000
Child care workers	250,000
Maintenance repairers	230,000
Teachers, Elementary School	220,000

Occupations having the largest numerical increase in employment from 1994-2005, by level of education and training, include:

First-Professional Degree:
  Lawyers
  Physicians
  Clergy
  Chiropractors
  Dentists

Doctoral Degree:
  College and university faculty
  Biological scientists
  Medical scientists
  Mathematicians

Master's Degree:
  Management analysts
  Counselors
  Speech-language pathologists and audiologists
  Psychologists
  Operations research analysts

Bachelor's Degree:
  Systems analysts
  Teachers, secondary school
  Teachers, elementary school
  Teachers, special education
  Social workers

Associate's Degree:
    Registered nurses
    Paralegals
    Radiologic technologiests and technicians
    Dental hygienists
    Medical records technicians

Occupational Outlook Handbook, U.S. Department of Labor, Bureau of Labor Statistics, 1996–1997 edition.

Interested in more details? If you'd like to find out more about projections and detail on the labor force, economic growth, industry and occupational employment, consult the November 1995 *Monthly Labor Review; The Employment Outlook: 1994–2005,* BLS Bulletin 2472. Or try the fall 1995 *Occupational Outlook Quarterly.* For more information about employment change, job openings, earnings, unemployment rates, and training requirements by occupation, consult *Occupational Projections and Training Data, 1996 Edition,* BLS Bulletin 2471.

CHAPTER 17

Insurance

Did you know that nearly one in every twelve dollars spent in the United States today pays for insurance? Did you know that the insurance industry employs 1.5 million people, 20 times more than the IRS and three times more than the U.S. Postal Service? Insurance is big business for a reason. Financial loss is a risk everyone faces, and you need to make some basic decisions about protecting yourself and your lifestyle.

Identify your financial risks. Start with a survey of the things you own. Then assign an estimated replacement value to each one. You'll need insurance to give you financial protection from loss by theft or fire of these belongings:

Your Assets   **Estimated Replacement Value**

Your home and furnishings:

_____   _____

_____   _____

_____   _____

_____   _____

Electronic equipment:

_____   _____

_____   _____

_____   _____

_____   _____

Jewelry:

_____ _____

_____ _____

_____ _____

_____ _____

Other personal property:

_____ _____

_____ _____

_____ _____

_____ _____

Next, consider your vehicles. Your vehicles pose two kinds of risks. First, you might lose them through theft or fire. Second, as the owner of a vehicle, you are exposed to additional risk of loss from damage or lawsuits resulting from accident or injury:

Your Assets   **Estimated Replacement Value**

Automobiles:

_____ _____

_____ _____

_____ _____

_____ _____

Recreational vehicles and equipment:

_____ _____

_____ _____

_____ _____

_____ _____

Other:

_____   _____
_____   _____
_____   _____
_____   _____

Now, take a small leap of faith and describe your health. Yes, that's right. If you've seen a health professional for any reason at all in the past five years, describe the circumstances. If you haven't, then describe your excellent health:

Your health:

_____
_____
_____
_____

Finally, describe your career goals and your estimated annual earnings. Multiply your estimated annual earnings by ten, twenty and forty years:

Your career goals:

_____
_____
_____
_____

Estimated annual earnings: ×**10:**   ×**20:**   ×**40:**
_____   _____   _____   _____

You have just inventoried your basic exposure to financial disaster. This is where professional financial planners start, and so should you. Your risk of loss falls into one of five fundamental categories: automobile, property, health, disability, and death. After describing your assets in each category, quantify the potential for financial loss as accurately as possible. Of course, you cannot possibly be 100 percent accurate. But you can estimate the most likely losses.

How Much Risk Should You Keep?

Your first decision involves the concept of risk. How much financial loss are you willing to absorb personally? Take a look at each category you described. If you lost it all, could you do without it altogether? Or could you easily replace it out of your savings or current income? If the thought of replacing it seems an unacceptable burden, then you are a prime candidate for transferring your risk of loss to an insurance carrier.

Rule #1: Cover the "What Ifs"

What if you were diagnosed with a serious disease that necessitated lengthy, expensive hospitalization? What if you were disabled and unable to earn a living? What if you were in an accident and injured others? What if your place was broken into and everything of value was stolen? What if . . . ? Your first step is to consider potential catastrophes and safeguard yourself financially. Then, within each category, consider how comprehensive each policy should be. How many and what type of events are covered? Think through the details. What if you were robbed? Does your contents insurance cover your jewelry for cost, depreciated cost, or replacement value? Do you need proof of theft? Do you need proof of value? What if it's lost and not stolen? What if . . . ?

Rule #2: Don't Sweat the Small Stuff

Everyone has different values and a different appetite for risk. Perhaps you drive a hand-me-down clunker and the thought of losing it is not that big of a deal to you. Or perhaps your car was brand, spanking new as a graduation gift and is your single most important possession. In fact, you would be financially devastated if you lost it. The insurance coverage you purchase in each of these scenarios should be vastly different. Take some time to think about how you define the "small stuff," that is, the financial risk you are willing to bear yourself.

Policies come in all shapes and sizes. Many fine references are available to walk you through the specifics of each type and to give you guidance on how to evaluate the pros and cons. Once you have familiarized yourself with the basics, you are ready to talk to a reputable insurance professional about the cost/benefit trade-offs of your protection choices.

How to Pick a Reputable Insurance Agent

The financial professionals you choose to be on your team are an important part of your overall financial security. You want them to grow with you over time and help you make the best decisions for you as your life circumstances change. You want to be able to rely upon their professional knowledge, judgment, advice, and customer service. You want to have confidence in the financial stability of the companies they represent, and their ability to pay claims when the time comes. After all, that's why you buy insurance; so it's there when you need it. Consider these important aspects of choosing an insurance professional:

- Ask financially successful friends and family whom they recommend, and whom they don't. Get as many different recommendations as you can.

- Set an appointment to interview the agent. Find out how long they've been in the business and how long they intend to be in it. Ask what they like about it as well as what they don't like. Ask for professional references. Really call them.

- Ask each agent about the financial integrity of the carriers they represent. Find out about their track record with claims. Ask about their turnaround time on claims.

- Insurance companies' financial stability is rated and published annually by A. M. Best, Moody's, and Standard & Poor's. Ask your agent for a copy of these ratings or look in your local library for comparative reports. Caveat: Each of these rating systems are different.

AUTOMOBILE INSURANCE

Car insurance may be the most expensive and most used coverage for young adults. If you're under 25, your premiums can easily be double or triple those of older adults. But you can take the reins and curb some of these costs while protecting yourself effectively. Here are the absolute basics—the very least you need to know to get started to ask the right questions for your individual situation:

Types of Coverage

Most people need a comprehensive policy with six types of coverage:

Collision: This type of coverage pays for repairs to your car caused by collision.

Comprehensive physical damage: This covers repairs to your car due to other causes.

Bodily injury liability: This pays for someone else's injury or death when your car is at fault.

Property damage liability: This type pays for property damage and legal bills when your car is at fault.

Medical payments: This type of coverage pays medical expenses as a result of your accident.

Uninsured motorists: This type pays when you are in an accident with an uninsured driver.

State laws govern coverage requirements and minimums, as well as "fault" and "right-to-sue" parameters. Get the details from your insurance agent and ask "what-if" questions.

Premiums

Premiums vary widely by location, age, sex, and type of car. In fact, rates often fluctuate by as much as 50 percent. You are wise to shop around and get quotes from many different agents and carriers.

Ask for any of these discounts that apply:

- Good grades
- Nonsmoker/nondrinker
- Driver's education
- Air bags
- Antilock brakes
- Antitheft devices

Lowering your deductible will lower your premiums. Decide what cost/benefit trade makes sense for you. Take the highest deductibles you feel comfortable with.

If you have homeowner's insurance, it often makes sense to combine your homeowner's insurance with your automobile insurance. You may get a better rate on both.

PROPERTY INSURANCE

You probably either rent or own. In either case, your personal property is at risk. If you own, then you will also insure the dwelling. Misleading as it is, the term homeowner's insurance applies to coverage for both renting and owning. The least you need to know:

- Replacement value insurance is the most likely kind of coverage to protect you from loss on the dwelling and your contents. You need a "replacement cost endorsement" rider added to your policy. This will cost about 10 percent more, and is usually well worth it.

- Make sure you know how the insurance company establishes replacement value. Find out what documentation you need for the existence and value of your assets.

- Specific items of personal property, such as expensive jewelry, may require an additional "personal articles floater" to pay replacement value.

- Carefully check the "exclusions" section of your policy to find out what is specifically not covered. You may get a rider at an additional expense to cover items you feel must be covered.

- Your insurance carrier is required to pay no more than the actual total amount stated in the policy. As you acquire assets, make sure that your policy amount is increased as needed to cover the total potential loss.

- Homeowner's insurance on the home you own automatically includes some standard liability coverage for damage to property (i.e., your child throws a ball through the neighbor's window) and medical payments to others (i.e., someone sues you after slipping on your sidewalk). However, renter's insurance may not. Check carefully.

HEALTH INSURANCE

There is no such thing as a standard health insurance policy or standard coverage. The insurance industry differentiates a "basic plan" from a "major medical plan." However, most group and individual policies offer both. The minimum you need to know:

- Basic plans cover hospital, surgical, and physicians' expenses. This includes some portion of room and board, nursing, drugs, lab, x-rays, certain surgical procedures, and physicians' fees.

- Major medical picks up where basic coverage ends. It may pick up extra days and/or extra expenses not covered in your basic policy.

- "Usual, customary, and reasonable" limitations may apply. Be careful. Your physician or hospital may ask you to sign a commitment to personally pay the uncovered excess.

- Plans typically pay 80 to 100 percent of your covered medical expenses over a base deductible amount. The amount you pay is called coinsurance. Know the total amount of coinsurance and deductible you may be required to pay in any given year.

- Know what is specifically not covered.

- Health Maintenance Organizations (HMOs) give you a choice of coverages for a flat monthly fee. Most require you to use their professional and facilities except in extreme emergencies.

- Preferred Provider Organizations (PPOs) offer a network of providers and work much like an HMO. PPOs generally offer a wider choice of professionals.

- Questions to ask HMOs and PPOs:

  - What type of prior authorization is required, and when?
  - What out of town treatment for accidents and emergencies is covered?
  - If so, what are the notification requirements?
  - What if you need a specialist not retained in the network?

- Regardless of the type of coverage you have, pay attention to deductibles, exclusions, and payment limits.

- If you lose your coverage because of termination or reduction of hours through an employer, the Comprehensive Omnibus Budget Reconciliation Act of 1986 (COBRA) requires employers of 20 or more to offer continued coverage for up to 18 months. The cost of the policy may be transferred to the employee.

DISABILITY INSURANCE

Fact: One year of disability can wipe out ten or more years of savings. Considering that your ability to earn a living is the most valuable asset you will ever have, disability insurance is imperative to your financial security. You must insure your paycheck. The minimum you need to know:

- The industry standard for short-term disability is 26 weeks. Long-term plans usually require medical qualification.

- If your company does not offer a disability plan, you may purchase an individual policy. But you must be employed to be eligible.

- You will most likely need enough coverage to replace 60 to 70 percent of your gross income.

- Rates vary with the risk factors associated with your job. For example, roofers pay lots more than clerical workers.

- Make sure that your policy is noncancellable as long as you pay your premiums.

- Avoid policies that pay only if you are totally disabled.

- Comparison shop until you've found the best policy and price for you.

LIFE INSURANCE

You may not need or want life insurance. But it is certainly worth considering:

- You may not necessarily want life insurance if you have no dependents—that is, no spouse or children. Or, if you have no considerable assets and/or no debts.

- You may want life insurance if you simply don't have the financial resources to pay for a funeral when you die (If this is the case, consider a simple "burial policy").

- Or, if you have dependents, you will certainly want to provide for their living after your death.

- Purchase enough coverage to provide 75 percent of your current annual pay, or 100 percent of your dependents' living expenses.

- Term insurance is usually adequate for all but the very wealthy. It covers the financial risk, but does not act as a savings account.

- Cash value insurance builds a savings account in addition to death benefits. It is usually much more expensive than term insurance and geared for the long-term investor.

- As you get older, the cost of a new policy increases.

CHAPTER 18

Investing for Your Future

Years ago, the American dream seemed simple: Get a good job with good benefits and a good retirement plan, settle down, buy a house and watch your net worth grow. Well, that's not reality anymore. (And it probably wasn't that simple even then.)

Reality today is that most employers don't offer good benefits and good retirement plans. And Social Security may not be around long enough to pay your benefits. If it is, there won't be nearly enough to meet your needs 40 years from now. In any event, it is up to you to secure your retirement to your comfort level. That's achieved through sound, consistent investments.

Before you jump into an investment strategy, respected financial planners recommend that you spend a few minutes mapping out your individual situation. Just as you would ponder and plan a vacation, your financial future deserves your undivided attention. Think of it: When you discuss a vacation, you actually consider things like what kind of comforts (or adventures) you want, how much money you have, how much time you can take, and what it will take to get there (fly? drive?). Then you put a plan together. You want a relaxing ocean retreat, so you spend $500 to go to Florida for four days. You'll have to drive, leaving Thursday at 4 P.M., heading south on I-24. And so on.

Your financial life deserves a similar focus. How much money do you make or have now? What are your dreams for wealth accumulation? When do you want to have it? What will it take to get there? Answering these questions may not seem important to you now, but if you wait until you need it, it's way too late. Americans today face intimidating odds against financial success. At age 65:

2%   Achieve financial independence
23% Must continue to work
75% Are destitute

Financial planners have studied these statistics to determine why only two percent of all Americans are financially successful. The results suggest six main reasons people fail financially:

1. Failure to develop a winning attitude (If you think you can't, you're right.)
2. Procrastination
3. No goals
4. Ignorance about what money must do to accomplish their goals (lack of understanding of investments and inflation)
5. Failure to safeguard assets and insure against the unexpected (lack of insurance)
6. Failure to understand and apply tax laws

The overriding message: Believe you can, learn the basics, set realistic goals, work a realistic plan now, and protect your foundation. You will be able to start with the information in these chapters. Then keep learning. It's a life-long quest, one step at a time. Your challenge is easier the sooner you begin.

For example, suppose you invested just $100 each month and earned a 12 percent return. If you begin at age 25, your investment will grow to $485,185 by the time you reach age 55. However, if you wait until you turn 40 to start investing that same $100 each month at 12 percent, your account will only grow to $89,323 by age 55. If you're counting on that $89,323 for retirement, how far will it go? To avoid that trap, start working your plan now.

THE EFFECTS OF INFLATION

Prices seem to go up every year. It's fairly predictable, and it's an important factor in your investment plan. Consider these average consumer prices:

	1970	1980	Today
Loaf of white bread	.23	.43	1.50
Man's haircut	2.50	4.25	20.00
Regular gas—10 gallons	3.48	9.68	12.90
Pack of cigarettes	.37	.62	2.00
Day at hospital (semiprivate room)	47.00	134.00	357.00
New car	3,400.00	6,910.00	19,500.00

| Woman's skirt | 12.00 | 28.00 | 40.00 |
| New house | 25,600.00 | 64,000.00 | 108,400.00 |

Now consider what inflation actually does to your purchasing power. One thousand dollars today will purchase much less in the future. By factoring in a 5 percent inflation rate each year, your $1,000 will buy these equivalents in the future:

Today	10 Years	20 Years	30 Years	40 Years
$1,000	$613	$376	$231	$142

Good investments will earn at least 5 percent. That means that you can maintain your purchasing power by building your account balance. If your investment account earns only 5 percent, here's what you will need in that account to maintain your purchasing power of $1000 today:

Today	10 Years	20 Years	30 Years	40 Years
$1,000	$1,628	$2,653	$4,321	$7,628

THE 12 PERCENT TARGET

The 12 Percent Target is your weapon against inflation. More important than that, it moves you ahead of the game and enables you to grow your investment account. Suppose you're earning 5 percent on your savings, after taxes. Assuming a 5 percent inflation rate, your net growth in purchasing power is zero. Your savings are simply maintaining your purchasing power. This is good, but you can do better than that.

By achieving a 12 percent annual return on your investment, you begin to build wealth. Now you have a net return of 7 percent. By reinvesting your earnings, you can double your money in about ten years. Not bad!

YOUR EARNING POWER

During your lifetime you will earn a great deal of money. The big challenge to financial security can be expressed very simply. How much of it can you keep?

Earnings

Monthly	10 Years	20 Years	30 Years	40 Years
$1,000	120,000	240,000	360,000	480,000
2,000	240,000	480,000	720,000	960,000
3,000	360,000	720,000	1,080,000	1,440,000
4,000	480,000	960,000	1,440,000	1,920,000
5,000	600,000	1,200,000	1,800,000	2,400,000
10,000	1,200,000	2,400,000	3,600,000	4,800,000

By setting aside a portion of your income each and every month, you begin to build the foundation. And with effective investing, you can accumulate much more than you earn.

CONSIDER YOUR SITUATION

Before plunging into any investment commitments, take time to assess your individual situation. Put it in writing, no matter how silly that seems. You should review and revise your plan periodically. A written plan makes your job easier. Answer the following questions:

- What financial goals do you have and when do you need the money?
- How many years do you have to save?
- Do you have a budget for your expenditures?
- How much money can you earn?
- How can you save more money?
- What is your appetite for risk?
- Can you manage your own investments, or do you need professional advice?
- What is the inflation rate?
- What returns are investments offering now?

What Are Your Goals?

Take a few moments to rank the following financial goals from 1 (most important) to 10:

_____Buy a house
_____Start a business
_____Increase standard of living
_____Increase net worth by___%
_____Financial security at retirement
_____Pay off debts
_____Save for children's college education
_____Reduce tax burden
_____Guard against unexpected financial burdens
_____Other _____

With this information, you have begun to identify your goals. When you get more specific, you can quantify real financial goals and make saving and investment decisions that will accomplish them. For instance, if you want to start a business, you must determine what kind of business, how much money you must have to fund it until it turns a profit, and when you need the money. Now you have a quantifiable financial goal. Quantifying all your financial goals requires careful consideration. Give some thought to seeking out a trusted, experienced friend or financial advisor for guidance.

THE INVESTMENT PYRAMID

Investing is risky. And scary. You can lose your hard-earned money almost overnight if you make mistakes or uninformed decisions. So it's easy to get overwhelmed and give up or avoid the whole thing. But you don't have to be a stock broker or financial planner to get started. Smart money managers start at the ground floor and build a financial foundation slowly and consistently. They start with the basics, and so can you.

Investing may be thought of as a pyramid. You build the foundation with the most stable, secure investments at the bottom, in the biggest proportion:

Third layer: High risk
Speculative stocks (less than $5 per share); Junk bonds and junk bond mutual funds; stock options; commodities; raw land; limited partnerships; precious metals; and collectibles

Second layer: Growth
Bonds and bond income mutual funds; common and preferred stocks; and stock mutual funds (also called equity mutual funds)

First layer: Conservative "foundation"
All federally insured bank accounts, including certificates of deposit (CDs), checking, savings, and money market accounts; all U.S. Treasury investments, including T-bills, T-notes, and T-bonds; series EE savings bonds; taxable and tax-free money market mutual funds; and tax-sheltered annuities

The pyramid approach suggests that you must have a solid base of diversified investments in the bottom layer to build a sound foundation. This is where you start, and you add layers as you go. The second layer increases risk, and increases return. It should be smaller than the bottom layer. Finally, the top layer is the smallest, with the most risk. Investors can more easily lose their investment.

The pyramid serves as a conceptual model. The specific investments must be designed to fit your individual situation, risk profile, and personal financial goals. The types and amounts within each layer will change over time, as your situation changes, the economy changes, your financial resources change, and your commitments change. The pyramid is different for everyone.

Many fine investment resources are available for more extensive information about each type of investment. Spending time learning about the various categories and choices within the categories is extremely important.

INVESTMENT TIPS

To help get you started on your search for solid investments, a few key points can help lead you in the right direction. Take these tips to heart when reading, researching, and establishing your foundation. Heeding this advice will take you leagues beyond the typical beginner. In fact, some of these tips are included in the bill by financial advisors when charging clients big hourly fees:

IRA

One of the best investments to start with is an Individual Retirement Account (IRA). If you qualify, your annual $2,000 (maximum) contribution is tax-free. If you're in a 28 percent tax bracket, you save $560 in taxes that year. Be sure to get all the details, because if you withdraw the money, you will have to pay those taxes plus an early withdrawal penalty.

401(k)

Many employers sponsor a plan that allows you to invest pre tax dollars. The money grows tax-deferred until you take it out. This allows you to increase your returns substantially, and is highly desirable, particularly if your employer also contributes. Make this a priority if it is available to you. Contribute the maximum amount.

Mutual Funds

Mutual Funds allow you to achieve diversification of your portfolio without having to commit a lot of money. It's best to start with "no-load" funds in a particular family. Work with a firm that allows you to exchange for free via the telephone.

Common Stock

When you purchase shares, you become a (fractional) owner of the company. Follow the company's reports and learn all you can about the industry and the company's performance. This is what drives the fortunes of the company, and the price of the shares. Your goal, of course, is to buy low and sell high.

Bonds

When you purchase bonds, you are actually loaning the company money, in return for an interest payment. Market interest rates and bond prices move in opposite directions.

Treasury Issues

Provide you a safe, fixed income, but no potential for growth.

Variable Annuities

Often provide tax-sheltered growth, but impose surrender charges and high annual fees.

Options and Commodities

If you can afford to lose a lot of money, you may be intrigued with the higher reward potential. Only for the highly knowledgeable investor.

Real Estate Investments

Real Estate Investment Trusts (REITs) are traded on the stock exchange and offer participation in the potential capital gains without the headaches of managing properties.

Limited Partnerships

May be a thing of the past for smart investors. Most cannot be easily resold and should therefore be avoided.

come to us for the best prep

about KAPLAN

EDUCATIONAL CENTERS

"How can you help me?"

From childhood to adulthood, there are points in life when you need to reach an important goal. Whether you want an academic edge, a high score on a critical test, admission to a competitive college, funding for school, or career success, Kaplan is the best source to help get you there. One of the nation's premier educational companies, Kaplan has already helped millions of students get ahead through our legendary courses and expanding catalog of products and services.

"I have to ace this test!"

The world leader in test preparation, Kaplan will help you get a higher score on standardized tests such as the SSAT and ISEE for secondary school, PSAT, SAT, and ACT for college, the LSAT, MCAT, GMAT, and GRE for graduate school, professional licensing exams for medicine, nursing, dentistry, and accounting, and specialized exams for international students and professionals.

Kaplan's courses are recognized worldwide for their high-quality instruction, state-of-the-art study tools and up-to-date, comprehensive information. Kaplan enrolls more than 150,000 students annually in its live courses at 1,200 locations worldwide.

"How can I pay my way?"

As the price of higher education continues to skyrocket, it's vital to get your share of financial aid and figure out how you're going to pay for school. Kaplan's financial aid resources simplify the often bewildering application process and show you how you can afford to attend the college or graduate school of your choice.

KapLoan, The Kaplan Student Loan Information Program,* helps students get key information and advice about educational loans for college and graduate school. Through an affiliation with one of the nation's largest student loan providers, you can access valuable information and guidance on federally insured parent and student loans. Kaplan directs you to the financing you need to reach your educational goals.

"Can you help me find a good school?"

Through its admissions consulting program, Kaplan offers expert advice on selecting a college, graduate school, or professional school. We can also show you how to maximize your chances of acceptance at the school of your choice.

"But then I have to get a great job!"

Whether you're a student or a grad, we can help you find a job that matches your interests. Kaplan can assist you by providing helpful assessment tests, job and employment data, recruiting services, and expert advice on how to land the right job. Crimson & Brown Associates, a division of Kaplan, is the leading collegiate diversity recruiting firm helping top-tier companies attract hard-to-find candidates.

Kaplan has the tools!

For students of every age, Kaplan offers the best-written, easiest-to-use books. Our growing library of titles includes guides for academic enrichment, test preparation, school selection, admissions, financial aid, and career and life skills.

Kaplan sets the standard for educational software with award-winning, innovative products for building study skills, preparing for entrance exams, choosing and paying for a school, pursuing a career, and more.

Helpful videos demystify college admissions and the SAT by leading the viewer on entertaining and irreverent "road trips" across America. Hitch a ride with Kaplan's *Secrets to College Admission* and *Secrets to SAT Success*.

Kaplan offers a variety of services online through sites on the Internet and America Online. Students can access information on achieving academic goals; testing, admissions, and financial aid; careers; fun contests and special promotions; live events; bulletin boards; links to helpful sites; and plenty of downloadable files, games, and software. Kaplan Online is the ultimate student resource.

Want more information about our services, products,
or the nearest Kaplan educational center?

HERE

Call our nationwide toll-free numbers:

1-800-KAP-TEST

(for information on our live courses, private tutoring and admissions consulting)

1-800-KAP-ITEM

(for information on our products)

1-888-KAP-LOAN*

(for information on student loans)

Connect with us in cyberspace:

On AOL, keyword "Kaplan"

On the Internet's World Wide Web, open "http://www.kaplan.com"

Via E-mail, "info@kaplan.com"

Write to:

**Kaplan Educational Centers
888 Seventh Avenue
New York, NY 10106**